500

asian dishes

500
asian dishes

the only compendium of asian dishes you'll ever need

Ghillie Başan

SELLERS

PUBLISHING

A Quintet Book

Published by Sellers Publishing, Inc.
161 John Roberts Road, South Portland, Maine 04106
For ordering information:
(800) 625-3386 Toll Free
(207) 772-6814 Fax
Visit our Web site: www.sellerspublishing.com
E-mail: rsp@rsvp.com

ISBN: 978-1-4162-0573-9
Library of Congress Control Number: 2010920878
QTT.THTA

This book was conceived, designed, and produced by
Quintet Publishing Limited
6 Blundell Street
London N7 9BH
United Kingdom

Project Editor: Martha Burley
Editorial Assistant: Holly Willsher
Food Stylist: Gizzi Erskine
Photographer: Ian Garlick
Art Director: Michael Charles
Managing Editor: Donna Gregory
Publisher: James Tavendale

10 9 8 7 6 5 4 3 2 1

Printed in China by 1010 Printing International Ltd.

Getty image appears on page 11 © Noe Montes/Getty.
iStock image appears on page 24.
Shutterstock images appear on pages 17; 18; 23; 27; 30; 33; 35;
41; 47.
Stock Food images appear on pages 79 © Cazals; Jean / StockFood;
84 © Eising, Susie M. / StockFood; 93 © Cazals; Jean / StockFood;
96 © Eising, Susie M. / StockFood.

contents

introduction

Asian cuisine is fusion cooking. With the ancient Chinese influence of civilization and cultivation at its root, it could be said that the collective Asian culinary culture is one that is founded on a balance of flavors, well-being, refinement, and artful presentation peppered with a flamboyant history of migration, early empires, trade routes, and colonization, all of which have contributed to the distinct differences between the individual countries. As these countries have evolved and traded together for millennia, the cuisine of the region is the best example of genuine "fusion" cooking in the world.

Geographically, the continent of Asia spreads across a vast chunk of the world, stretching from Turkey in the west to the far shores of Japan and the Philippines in the east. From a cultural and culinary perspective, though, Asia can be divided into three main categories: the Middle East; India and Pakistan; and the East and Southeast. However, when we talk about Asian people and their cooking, we are generally referring to the cuisines of East and Southeast Asia—principally China, Taiwan, Korea, Japan, Vietnam, Cambodia, Laos, Thailand, Malaysia, Singapore, Brunei, Indonesia, and the Philippines, with Mongolia and Burma on the fringes.

Asian cuisine was undoubtedly shaped by the ancient trade routes, which passed through Southeast Asia from China to India and the Arab world and subsequently to Europe. With people and goods traveling from east to west and west to east, new ingredients and cooking methods were introduced, as well as different religions. For example, Islamic influences arrived from the Middle East and India; Hinduism also came from India; the European traders and colonizers brought Christianity; the Chinese spread their ancient philosophies and the art of cultivating of rice; and spices such as coriander, cumin, cinnamon, and cloves spread throughout the region. In the 16th century, the European explorers from Portugal and Spain brought foods from the New World, such as tomatoes, peanuts, corn, and chiles, all of which grew with ease in the tropical soil and were swiftly incorporated into the developing cuisine. The Dutch, British, French, Portuguese, and Spanish also made a culinary impact as they colonized different parts of the South Seas, while a thread of Indian culinary influence penetrated most of Southeast Asia. The most dominant influence of all, however, was the Chinese one, which is at the root of all Asian cooking.

Central to all Asian cooking is rice and a wok, two principal influences from China. Rice, whether it is the grain itself or in the form of rice noodles or rice wrappers, is the staple food of all the diverse cultures, and a meal without it would not be considered a meal at all. Other Chinese influences evident in Asian cooking are stir-fried and steamed dishes, noodles, savory and sweet dumplings, lightly cooked vegetables wrapped in rice wrappers, delicately flavored light soups, braised dishes, and the use of sauces, such as soy, in the cooking as well as for dipping sauces and relishes for serving.

When it comes to the Asian cooking method, the majority of time is spent in the preparation of ingredients, such as the chopping and marinating. The cooking is relatively quick and the dish is intended to be served and eaten right away—from the wok to the bowl. The shape and texture of the ingredients, whether they are cut into cubes, matchsticks, or shredded, is crucial to the overall cooking time and enjoyment of a dish. Oven-roasting and baking seldom take place, as most dishes are stir-fried in a wok, grilled over charcoal, or steamed. The simple utensils common to all the culinary cultures of the region include a wok, a bamboo steamer, grinding equipment such as a mortar and pestle or a grinding stone, and a sharp cleaver for chopping.

The majority of Asian dishes are potentially snack dishes, but when served as a meal they are generally presented as a buffet and everyone takes what they like and adds it to their individual bowl of rice or noodles. The reason for this is to divide and balance the "fan"— grains and other starch foods known as staples, such as noodles, rice, and bread—with the "cai," the cooked meat and vegetables. To achieve the perfect balance, an Asian meal requires the five elements of ancient Chinese cuisine—a blend of color, aroma, flavor, shape, and texture.

Spicy and tangy, sweet and fruity, sour and fiery are the principal notes you will encounter as you embark on an Asian voyage of soy sauce spiked with chile and garlic; noodles in coconut milk with lemongrass and ginger; tamarind and cilantro with shrimp; tender beef flavored with star anise; chicken braised with tiger lilies; refreshing salads of mango, pineapple, bean sprouts, bamboo shoots, and lime; pearly white lychee sorbet; and honey-sweetened infusions of Asian pear, persimmon, and pandanus leaf. The exotic flavors of gingerroot, lemongrass, chile, cilantro, tamarind, mango, papaya, coconut, and lime are at the heart of this vibrant and creative cuisine that surprises and delights with every bite. In a nutshell, this is the essence of Asian cooking.

china

Chinese cooking cannot really be defined as one style, as it is divided into regional styles relating to this vast country's geographical differences. However, although the styles may vary, they all have a common base of flavorings, methods, and techniques, which are at the root of all the neighboring culinary cultures and are what we in the West regard as Chinese cooking. For example, throughout China, fresh gingerroot, soy sauce, and scallions are used in the majority of dishes, which are generally stir-fried and served with noodles or steamed rice. A great deal of importance is attached to the preparation of dishes, such as the chopping and marinating, and this is where most of the time is spent, as the actual cooking is comparatively quick. The cooking utensils, which have also spread to the neighboring countries, are very basic, essentially consisting of a wok, a basket for steaming, a pot for noodles, and a sharp cleaver.

At the heart of all Chinese cooking is the philosophy of yin-yang, which is basically the interaction of the two opposing forces of the universe; the female, dark and cold (yin), represented by the moon, and the male, light and hot (yang), represented by the sun. This duality also applies to food in order to maintain a balance in the body and is taken into account when preparing a meal. Yin foods, such as watery vegetables and fruit, have a cooling effect on the blood, so they must be balanced by warming yang foods, such as meats and hot spices. Also, hand in hand with the yin-yang philosophy is the Chinese system of five elements—earth, wood, fire, metal, and water—which play an important role in the food culture, as the number five is perpetuated in various ways, such as five-spice powder and the five fundamental flavors: sweet, sour, bitter, hot, and salty. The philosophy of yin-yang, combined with those five fundamental flavors, is at the root of all Asian cooking.

korea

Primarily of Mongolian descent, Koreans have a rich culture with an elaborate system of etiquette and a bold cuisine. The political division of the country also corresponds with the geographical and climatic factors, resulting in more food being produced in the fertile plains of South Korea. Similar to Vietnam, there are two distinct types of cooking—the home cooking of the traditional family and the elaborate court cuisine.

Koreans follow the Chinese rule of five traditional flavors with salt provided by soy sauce or bean paste; sweet by beet sugar, sweet potatoes, and honey; hot by chiles and mustard; sour generally by vinegar; and bitter by gingerroot. The Koreans also follow their own arrangement of five traditional colors: red, green, yellow, white, and black, although the latter is generally represented by gray or brown through the use of dried mushrooms. The methods and flavors used in Korean cooking display threads of Chinese influence with an emphasis on gingerroot, chile, mustard, scallions, garlic, soy sauce, vinegar, and sesame seeds. Beef, which is generally very finely sliced and marinated before cooking, is the most commonly consumed meat, although chicken and pork are popular too. The national pickled vegetables, kimchi, accompany most meals.

Like the Chinese, the Koreans often combine fish and shellfish with pork and poultry and they share a passion for seaweed with the Japanese. Other aspects of Japanese cooking mirrored in Korea include the raw fish "sushi" dishes and a tendency toward quality, not quantity, in the presentation of the food. In addition to the stir-fry method of the region, the Koreans also prepare many of their dishes over a charcoal grill. Traditionally, a meal consists of three to seven dishes, which are served with chopsticks but eaten from bowls with spoons.

A table at a Korean restaurant with a grill in the center

japan

Japan is perhaps best known outside the region for its meticulous preparation of food and its refined, artistic presentation. Portions are small and carefully arranged with an emphasis on color and texture. With mountainous islands and little space for agricultural plains, this method of eating has perhaps come about by necessity rather than choice—relying on quality rather than quantity. Of all the cuisines of this region, the Japanese one is perhaps the most distinct. Rather than blending herbs and spices with the ingredients to produce a full-flavored dish, the Japanese tend to cook ingredients individually, with an emphasis on texture. To compensate for the limited produce, presentation of the food is of utmost importance, with individual morsels exquisitely arranged to resemble a painting.

The early Japanese probably came from Siberia and developed a deep appreciation for nature, which later became a cult of worship and is still at the root of the cuisine through the incorporation of various plants. Seaweed plays a big role in the Japanese diet, which otherwise consists primarily of fish, vegetables, fruit, and rice. Unlike most of its neighbors, Japan's basic diet has been little affected by outside influences, apart from that of the Chinese (evident in the soy products, tea, rice, and the stir-fry method), and of the Portuguese, who introduced the technique of frying ingredients dipped in batter, resulting in the Japanese tempura.

The waters around the islands provide the Japanese with their daily fare: fish or shellfish, which is eaten both raw (sushi) and cooked at every meal, and seaweed, which is used as a wrapper, garnish, or stir-fried vegetable and as the basis of the ubiquitous stock, dashi. Other distinct features of Japanese cooking include miso, a savory paste made from fermented soy beans, which provides a unique flavor to a number of dishes; sake, the well-known rice wine; and mirin, a sweetened rice wine used in cooking and in marinades.

vietnam

Vietnam enjoys a delicate and complex cuisine. Its roots in Chinese cooking are combined with the finesse of the French and the influence of Indian spices in the south. The geographic split of this skinny country bears a strong impact on the regional differences in the cuisine. As the Vietnamese will point out, the country is shaped like a don ganh, the traditional bamboo pole slung over the shoulder with a basket of rice hanging from each end. These baskets represent the rice bowls of Vietnam—the Red River Delta in the north and the vast Mekong Delta in the south—connected by a mountainous spine. Stretching from tip to tip on the eastern side is just under 2,000 miles of coastline, which, in addition to the numerous flowing rivers and streams that carve up the land, provides Vietnam with such a volume of water that it has a steady supply of its two most important ingredients: rice and nuoc mam, fermented fish sauce.

Like the Thais and Cambodians, the Vietnamese enjoy wrapping lightly cooked ingredients in rice wrappers or lettuce leaves and serving them with pickled vegetables, fresh chiles, and dipping sauces. One of the distinct features of Vietnamese cooking lies in the French influence of savory pâtés and the inclusion of loaves of bread, instead of the ubiquitous rice and noodles.

While strolling through a Vietnamese market, the culinary influences come together in perfect harmony. First, there is the addictive aroma of pho, the Chinese-inspired noodle soup, emanating from a small wooden stall. Next to it is a wooden cart laden with warm, freshly baked baguette halves smeared with an aromatic, French-inspired pork pâté. Farther along is the mouthwatering lure of sweet, plump shrimp stir-fried in fragrant lemongrass and pungent Indian spices, all culminating in a splashy crescendo of the very Vietnamese nuoc mam or its tangier, piquant relative, nuoc cham.

The contrasting flavors and textures of sweet basil leaves, roasted peanuts, liberal quantities of garlic and ginger, perfumed mint, banana blossom, lotus seeds, and shredded green papaya contribute to a rich tapestry of exotic pleasure.

Two street vendors serve fresh food at a market in Hoi An, Vietnam

Fish drying out in a Cambodian village

cambodia

For most of its recent history, Cambodia has been shut off from the rest of the world, but that has begun to change and the cuisine is experiencing a revival. On the whole, the food of Cambodia is based on peasant dishes reflecting those of its neighbors—Thailand, Laos, and Vietnam—with the influence of Indian spices and the practice of wrapping ingredients in leaves. The Chinese influence in all these countries is evident in the rice preparations, tea, and the stir-fry method. The Cambodians particularly enjoy sour, acid tastes, generally obtained from tamarind extracts and fresh limes. Lemongrass and galangal are featured in many dishes and form the basis of the ubiquitous herbal paste, kroeung. Fish sauces and other preserved fish products are essential to Cambodian cuisine, as are jungle preparations such as meat or rice cooked in the hollow of bamboo stems over open fires, perhaps because of long periods of poverty and jungle living through the times of political turmoil and inhumane regimes.

The symbol of Cambodia is the sugar palm tree, which is used in the production of medicine, wine, and vinegar. The northeast of the country is mountainous and the east is covered with dense jungle, so the country's rice bowl is in the west and central lowlands, where other crops such as vegetables and maize are grown. The countryside markets offer a variety of livestock for the pot, including an unenviable selection of endangered animals and large, black, hairy spiders! Fish is caught mostly in the mighty Mekong River and the Tonle Sap Lake, which has the unusual feature of swelling when the Mekong rises and then draining when the level of the Mekong falls, making the lake a rich source of freshwater fish and the flooded land around it an ideal spawning ground.

thailand

Unlike the rest of Southeast Asia, Thailand was never colonized, so much of the population is indigenous and, apart from specific Chinese influences, the outside ones only skirt the surface of the culinary culture rather than form the roots. The Chinese influence has spread to Thailand in the form of steamed rice and noodles, both of which the Thais like to serve with their hot sauce (nam prik), tea, and the stir-frying method. Rice is the mainstay of most meals, although cassava and maize play a big role too. The interplay of flavors is a predominant feature of Thai cooking, with an emphasis on sour, salt, and sweet combined with the heat of chiles. Cilantro, coconut milk, palm sugar, kaffir limes, and basil are other predominant features that spill into parts of Malaysia, Laos, Burma, Cambodia, and Vietnam. Indian spices, such as turmeric, cardamom, and cinnamon, also play a role in this region.

The majority of the population is Buddhist, with minority groups of Muslims and Christians. The impact that Buddhism has made on the food of the region lies purely in its ritual role, with offerings made to the spirits and specially prepared food given to monks as alms. Thai funerals and weddings are celebrated with specific feasts. The royal court of Thailand has helped a great deal to put the cuisine of Thailand on the global culinary map, as many of the kings have written cookbooks and taken great pride in their cuisine. Perhaps the best-known features of Thai cuisine are the curries, gaeng, which are very hot and based on a spice paste that will color them red, green, or yellow. Thailand has also become one of the greatest rice-growing countries in the region and relies on rice for the export revenue. There are, therefore, many rituals attached to the planting and harvesting of rice, as it represents life.

malaysia & singapore

Although Malaysia and Singapore are politically separate, they are geographically united and include Brunei in their sphere. At the root of the cuisines of all three areas are Chinese, Malay, and Indian influences. The majority of Malaysia's population is Muslim, which has an effect on the cooking of the region, particularly in the prohibition of pork and the religious fasting and celebratory feasts. It is also in Malaysia and Singapore where the Indian influence is felt almost as strongly as the Chinese because of the great influx of Indian laborers during the colonial period.

Unique to Malaysia and Singapore is Nonya cooking, which is associated with the Chinese immigrants. The flavors of Nonya cooking are similar to many of the indigenous Malay and Indonesian traditions, such as chiles, shrimp paste, coconut milk, and occasionally Indian spices, but it is the use of noodles and pork in these dishes that makes them unique. Another unique characteristic of the cooking in Malaysia and Singapore is the use of a rempah—a spice mixture that is fried at the beginning of cooking to give the dish greater depth. The sambal, a spice mixture or relish employed during cooking or served with the cooked dish, and achar, a pickle or pickled vegetables served with the cooked dish, are common fare in this region. The ubiquitous satay dishes, which are really Asian kebabs prepared with small cuts of marinated meat, are also a familiar sight in the region, as well as in neighboring Thailand and Indonesia.

The cultural mix of Malaysia and Singapore is so diverse it reads like a recipe itself. The population of Malaysia is approximately 60 percent Malay, 26 percent Chinese, and 7 percent Indian, with a dash of Peranakan, Eurasian, Indonesian, and tribal influences, garnished with

A local market in Kelantan, Malaysia

Vietnamese, Japanese, Filipino, and Thai. In Singapore, on the other hand, the population is 76 percent Chinese, 15 percent Malay, and 6 percent Indian, with a drop of Peranakan, Eurasian, and Indonesia, sprinkled with Western influences.

Singapore is also one of the world's greatest entrepôts for spices, with an unrivaled variety available in the markets. What this all adds up to is one of the most colorful and exciting culinary scenes in the world, made all the more tangible with the fascinating tradition of hawker stalls, where food from all these cultures can be sampled in one place.

Newly planted rice seedlings in a rural area in Malaysia

indonesia

Once described as a "jeweled necklace" strung between Australia and the mainland of Southeast Asia, Indonesia is made up of more than 13,500 islands (only some of which have names) and includes Java, Bali, Sumatra, parts of Borneo, and parts of New Guinea. The population of Indonesia is distributed among more than 5,000 islands, which vary enormously in climate and soil, and some are even barely habitable.

Rice is the main staple, but in the eastern parts of Indonesia taro, cassava, and sago are the main staples. Fish is obviously abundant and forms the daily fare of the majority of the population, ranging from tuna, anchovies, milkfish, shellfish, catfish, and carp. Dried fish also is part of the daily fare, for flavoring dishes and to eat as snacks. Almost every dish is flavored with—or accompanied by—chiles. Indonesians love chiles and they tend to balance the fiery heat in dishes by adding a sweetness with sugar or fruit, or by a sourness derived from tamarind or lime. The principal flavors of Indonesian food are similar to those of its neighbors—tamarind, lemongrass, chiles, turmeric, and galangal or gingerroot. Many dishes resemble ones from Malaysia, and both regions rely heavily on a variety of sambals, which are fragrant or fiery spice pastes added to the dish while cooking, or served as a relish. One of the best-known Indonesian dishes is fried rice served with a fried egg on top.

The majority of Indonesia's population is Muslim, so the Islamic culinary restrictions, such as no consumption of pork or alcohol, are adhered to, but goat, lamb, and beef are popular. Islamic religious holidays and feasts are celebrated in much the same way as in other Muslim communities around the world, with an emphasis on Ramadam, the month of fasting. There is also a thriving Hindu population with its own culinary restrictions and feasts, centered around colorful curries and lots of chicken and vegetable dishes, as the sacred cow is not slaughtered for meat.

A harvest of coconuts on the ground in Bajawa, Indonesia

philippines

The islands of the Philippines, situated approximately 500 miles southeast of the Asian continent, are more compact than the islands that make up Indonesia. Of all the cuisines in the region, the Filipino one is the most diverse. Its visible roots are set in its complex history of Malay, Chinese, Spanish, Mexican, and American rulers and traders, peppered with Indian and Arab influences, particularly among the Muslim communities. Perhaps the greatest influence of all came from the Spanish colonial regime, with its conversion of the inhabitants to Catholicism and the inherent religious feasts, as well as the mix of Spanish and Mexican dishes, including paella and adobo and the introduction of olives, vinegar, and wine.

The Americans brought their tradition of convenience and fast foods such as sandwiches and burgers and ice cream. But, in spite of these outside influences, the Chinese roots are still strong, reflected in the stir-fry and noodle dishes, the popularity of rice wrappers and steamed rice, and the use of soy sauce and other Chinese sauces to flavor and serve with dishes.

As with most of this part of Asia, rice is the basis of all meals in the Philippines, but it is prepared in a variety of ways, ranging from the Chinese steamed and sticky rice versions to a variety of stir-fried and pilaf methods. Coconuts also feature heavily in the diet of the Filipinos. They are used to make coconut milk and vinegar; the flesh is used in a variety of sweet and savory dishes; and the leaves are used for wrapping morsels of meat or rice. Like Indonesia, the islands of the Philippines are blessed with a variety of fish and shellfish, which feature in daily fare but, unlike that of many of its neighbors, the diet of the Philippines features pork in a big way. Almost every family has a pig, and pork is the most popular meat for everyday food as well as the colorful Catholic celebratory feasts.

asian ingredients

The traditional Asian kitchen is vibrant and packed with flavor, relying on a variety of fresh ingredients. If we look at rice and fish as the Asian palette, then coconut milk, lemongrass, gingerroot, garlic, chiles, and cilantro are the paints. Add fermented and preserved flavorings, such as soy and fish sauces, delicately perfumed broths, and indigenous shoots and vegetables, and you will have stocked some of the essential ingredients found in every Asian kitchen.

rice

In Asia, there are three main groups of rice: long-grain, short-grain, and sticky "glutinous" rice. Long- and short-grain rice is employed daily in all Asian cooking. Often delicately scented, such as the fragrant jasmine variety, the grains should be dry, firm, and translucent when raw. Once cooked, the tender grains should turn white and fluff up easily with a fork while retaining a bite. Sticky or "glutinous" rice comes in both long- and short-grain varieties, both of which are soaked for several hours, sometimes overnight, before cooking to attain the thick "sticky" texture required. Rice is also distilled to make a dry wine, sake, and a sweet wine, mirin, and a sharp vinegar used for pickling raw vegetables.

noodles

Noodles play a prominent part in the cooking of Asia. If the main dish doesn't contain rice to provide the starch content of the meal, then it will consist of noodles. There are a variety of noodles principally made from rice, wheat, and egg. Noodles are eaten at all hours of the day, in a soup for breakfast, simply stir-fried for a quick and filling snack, or more elaborately compiled into a main dish with meat, fish, and vegetables.

spices, herbs & flavorings

While rice and noodles form the basis of everyday Asian cuisine, the spices, herbs, and flavorings paint the scenes. A dish would be unthinkable without a splash of soy sauce or a sprinkling of scallions—they add flavor, color, and texture.

chinese five-spice powder
Based on a mixture of five spices that represent the five basic flavors at the root of Chinese cooking—sweet, sour, bitter, hot, and salty—this powder is traditionally made up of star anise, cloves, fennel seeds, cinnamon, and Szechuan peppercorns. It is available in supermarkets and Asian markets.

chiles
Throughout Asia, the chiles most frequently used are the small, fiery, red and green "Thai bird" varieties. Bright colored and slender, they are also called "finger" chiles because of their shape. Fresh chiles are used liberally in the Asian kitchen, but they also are dried and ground to a powder or used to flavor oil.

fish sauce
Fermented fish sauce is a principal ingredient in Asian cooking, particularly in soups, stir-fries, marinades, and dipping sauces. It has a distinctive, pungent smell and, if used in moderation, it enhances the flavor of the dish it is added to. Bottles of fish sauce are available in most supermarkets and Asian stores.

galangal

A member of the ginger family, and similar in appearance, galangal is aromatic and pungent. Used in much the same way as ginger, galangal is used in spicy pastes and marinades, as well as in soups and curries. Fresh and dried galangal can be found in Asian markets.

garlic

Garlic has been used in the cooking of Asia since ancient times. Chopped or crushed, garlic is added liberally to stir-fries, curries, stews, and noodles. It is also used in its raw form to flavor pickles, marinades, sauces, and dips.

gingerroot

Indigenous to the Asian jungles, gingerroot is a great favorite in Asian cooking. Chopped or shredded, the juicy, sweet, and pungent flesh of fresh gingerroot is used liberally in stir-fries, stews, rice, pickles, steamed dishes, and puddings.

kaffir lime leaves

There is no real substitute for kaffir lime leaves, which lend a bitter, flowery note to soups and stews. They are available fresh or dried in Asian markets, and packets of dried leaves are available in most supermarkets.

lemongrass

Lemongrass is a woody, fibrous stalk that is sweet, floral, and lemony in flavor. It is pale yellowish-green in color, encased in a paperlike sheath. Once the outer layers have been removed, the lower part of the stalk and the bulb are chopped, pounded, or crushed and added to soups, stir-fries, curries, and marinades.

palm sugar

Widely used in Asian cooking, palm sugar is golden to toffee-brown in color with a distinctive flavor. Extracted from the sap of various palm trees, the sugar is usually sold in blocks, often referred to as "jaggery" in Asian stores.

pandanus leaf

Fruity-vanilla in taste, pandanus leaves are available fresh or dried in some Asian markets. The long, narrow leaves are tied together and bruised to release their unique flavor before being added to dishes.

soy sauce

Soy sauce is perhaps the most commonly used sauce in Asian cooking. It is used extensively in stir-fries, marinades, and dipping sauces. Plain and sweet versions are available in supermarkets and Asian stores. When buying soy sauce, it is important to look for natural brands containing fermented soy beans, wheat, yeast, and salt—avoid brands that contain caramel and coloring. For sweet soy sauces, look for Chinese hoisin sauce, prepared with fermented soy beans, vinegar, sugar, and garlic, or Indonesian sweet soy sauce, which is thick and dark and sweetened with palm sugar.

star anise

Star anise is the dried, star-shaped fruit of a slender evergreen tree that grows in Asia. The fruits are reddish-brown with a seed in each of the eight prongs of the star. Not related to anise seed, star anise lends a strong licorice flavor to a number of soups and stews.

tiger lily buds

Native to Asia, tiger lilies produce masses of buds, which are picked unopened and dried before use. Also known as "golden needles," as they are light golden in color, they are regarded as both a vegetable and herb. Ranging from 2 to 4 inches long, they are floral-scented and slightly earthy in flavor with mushroom overtones. Traditionally, before cooking, the buds are knotted in the center and soaked in water for about 30 minutes. This ensures that the lilies remain intact when cooked and that they retain a slightly chewy texture. Bags of dried, tangled buds are sold in Asian stores.

turmeric

Fresh turmeric is a knobbly root with fingers, similar in appearance to ginger, although dark brown in color with a bright orange flesh. The fresh root has a subtle, earthy taste and imparts a vibrant yellowy-orange color to dishes. It is also dried and ground to a deep yellow powder to give both flavor and color to dishes, marinades, spice mixes, and batters. Both fresh and dried turmeric are available in Asian markets. Dried turmeric is sold in most supermarkets as well.

vegetables

Raw, stir-fried, braised, pickled, or salted vegetables are worked into every meal in some manner in Asia. Almost every dish includes a few vegetables, but, in addition, there may be a vegetable side dish, salad, pickled vegetables, or leaves to wrap around the food. The main thing to remember is that an Asian meal must be balanced with vegetable, protein, and starch. Typical vegetables in the Asian kitchen include snake beans, daikon, bok choy, jicama, bamboo shoots, bean sprouts, winter melon, small eggplants, and mushrooms.

bamboo shoots

Fresh, pickled, or dried bamboo shoots are popular throughout Asia. The creamy-white, fresh shoots have a wonderful texture and flavor and are delicious in stir-fries and soups. Dried shoots require soaking before use and, once cooked, should retain a crunch and taste slightly sweet. Fresh shoots are available in Asian stores, but cans of cooked shoots, preserved in brine, can be bought in most supermarkets.

bean sprouts

Popular throughout Asia, bean sprouts can be eaten raw or added to many stir-fries and soups for their refreshing, crunchy bite. The most common sprouts come from mung beans and soy beans. Packets of mung bean sprouts are readily available in most supermarkets, but soy bean sprouts are generally found in Asian stores and some health food stores. Canned bean sprouts are sold in supermarkets, but try to use fresh whenever possible.

bok choy

This perennial, green, leafy cabbage has juicy white stems and crunchy dark green leaves. The tender stems of small cabbages are often eaten raw with a dipping sauce and the leaves are stir-fried quickly to retain the texture and flavor. Also known as "pak choi," bok choy is found in supermarkets and Asian markets.

daikon

White in color, this root vegetable looks very similar to a large carrot. Also known as Oriental white radish, it is crisp and juicy and ideal for salads and pickles, as well soups and stews. Daikon can be found in Asian markets.

jicama

Resembling a large turnip, this root vegetable has a delicate taste with a crunchy texture, similar to water chestnuts and lotus roots. It only needs to be peeled before use and cut into the desired chunks or slices for soups, salads, and stir-fries. Jicama can be found in most Asian stores, as well as Hispanic markets.

snake beans

These long, green beans, known as "snake beans," "chopstick beans," or "yard-long beans," are the immature pods of black-eyed peas and can measure up to 2 feet in length. Generally they are stir-fried with basic flavorings like garlic and ginger and served as a side dish, or added to soups and curries. Pencil-thin and dark or light green in color, they are available in Asian markets.

winter melon

Large, mild-flavored gourds, dark green winter melons have white flesh that tastes like a large zucchini. Prepared and cooked in much the same way as a pumpkin, winter melon is added to soups, stews, and stir-fries because the flesh absorbs the flavors of the dish. Winter melons are available in Asian markets.

fruit

In Asia seasonal fresh fruit is often served at the end of a meal to refresh the palate and aid the digestion, while sweet puddings and cakes are enjoyed as a snack at any time of the day. The variety of exotic, tropical fruits is astounding, including fresh coconut, banana, lychee, pineapple, mangosteen, mango, papaya, star fruit, jackfruit, guava, passion fruit, pomelo, dragon fruit, and the pungent durian.

bananas

Along with coconuts, bananas are the most widely used fruit in Asia. Ripe and unripe bananas are employed in sweet and savory dishes, while the blossom and hearts (sold in Asian markets) are tossed in salads and the leaves are used for wrapping around ingredients or as serving dishes.

coconut

The coconut is the most used fruit for both sweet and savory dishes throughout Asia. They are enjoyed both ripened and immature. The ripened ones are used for cooking and for making coconut milk, whereas the soft, jellylike flesh of the young ones is preferred for snacking on. Coconut milk is made by soaking grated coconut flesh in hot water and then squeezing it to extract the liquid. It is added to soups, curries, stir-fries, and sauces and is the basis of many sweet dishes. Cans of unsweetened coconut milk are sold in supermarkets and Asian stores. Coconut vinegar comes from the sap of the coconut palm, which is aired and left to sour so that it can be used as a vinegar.

sauces & dips

Pastes, marinades, dipping sauces, and garnishes

play a key role in the preparation and enjoyment of

Asian cooking. Served as an accompaniment to

most dishes, they provide the principal notes—spicy

and tangy, sweet and fruity, sour and fiery—the

essence of Asian cuisine.

malaysian chile relish

see variations page 61

This strong, fiery taste is typical of Malay cuisine, so this pungent chile condiment is served with almost every dish. A little spoonful seems to go with everything—chunks of bread, rice, broiled foods, and stir-fried vegetables. Malaysian, Thai, and Indonesian fermented shrimp pastes can be found in Asian markets and some supermarkets.

1 tbsp. shrimp paste
4 fresh red chiles, stalks and seeds removed
   (keep the seeds)
2 fresh kaffir lime leaves, spines removed, and
   shredded

1/4 tsp. salt
1/2 tsp. palm sugar
juice of 1 lime
1 lime, cut in wedges, to serve

In a small heavy pan, dry-roast shrimp paste until it is aromatic and crumbly. Then, using a mortar and pestle, grind roasted shrimp paste with chiles to form a paste. Grind in half the chile seeds and the lime leaves. Add salt and sugar, and stir in remaining chile seeds. Moisten with juice of 1 lime. Spoon relish into a small bowl and serve with wedges of lime to squeeze over it.

Serves 4

indonesian fiery peanut sauce

see variations page 62

This is a very popular dipping sauce for fried and broiled meats and steamed vegetables. Similar to the peanut sauces of Malaysia, Vietnam, and Thailand, it is always available at street stalls. To make an authentic peanut sauce, the peanuts must be very finely ground, which can be done in an electric blender.

1–2 tbsp. peanut or vegetable oil
1 shallot, peeled and finely chopped
2 cloves garlic, peeled and finely chopped
3/4 cup unsalted peanuts, finely ground
1 tbsp. Indonesian or Thai shrimp paste

1 tbsp. palm sugar
1 tbsp. tamarind paste
1 tbsp. Indonesian sweet soy sauce
1 tbsp. chili powder
1 1/4 cups water

Heat oil in a heavy pan, stir in shallot and garlic, and cook until golden. Add ground peanuts, shrimp paste, and sugar, and continue to fry for 3–4 minutes, until peanuts begin to color and release some of their oil.

Stir in tamarind paste, sweet soy sauce, and chili powder. Add water and bring mixture to a boil. Reduce heat and boil gently for 15–20 minutes, until mixture has reduced and thickened. Leave mixture to cool, then pour into an electric blender and whiz to a smooth sauce. It may be kept in refrigerator, covered, for a week.

Serves 4

filipino lime sauce

see variations page 63

This popular Filipino dipping sauce can be served with anything, but it is particularly delicious with fish and rice dishes. Made with the small kalamansi limes (calamondin oranges), it refreshes and enhances the flavor of many dishes.

4 tbsp. fish sauce
2 fresh kalamansi limes (calamondin oranges), squeezed

In a bowl, beat fish sauce with citrus juice until thoroughly blended. May be kept covered in the refrigerator for a day or two.

Serves 4

cambodian herbal paste

see variations page 64

This versatile herbal paste includes the three key components of Cambodian cooking—lemongrass, galangal, and turmeric. It is used to flavor many soups and stir-fries, and it is rubbed on meat and fish before grilling over charcoal.

2–3 lemongrass stalks, trimmed with outer
    leaves removed, and chopped
1 oz. fresh galangal, peeled and chopped
1 oz. fresh turmeric, peeled and chopped
6–8 garlic cloves, peeled and crushed

1 small onion, or 2 shallots, peeled and finely
    chopped
4 fresh kaffir lime leaves, ribs removed
1/2 tsp. coarse sea salt

Using a mortar and pestle, grind ingredients to a paste, adding a little water to bind. Or put all the ingredients in a blender with 1–2 tablespoons water and whiz until they form a paste.

Spoon paste into a jar or small bowl, and cover. May be kept in refrigerator for a week.

Makes about 2/3 cup

vietnamese dipping sauce

see variations page 65

This popular dipping sauce varies in sweet, sour, and fiery degrees, depending on the cook and the region. It can be served with everything from spring rolls to broiled meats and seafoods.

4 cloves garlic
2 fresh red chiles, with stem and seeds removed
3–4 tsp. palm sugar

juice of 1/2 lime
5 tbsp. water
4 tbsp. Vietnamese or Thai fish sauce

Using a mortar and pestle, grind garlic and chile with sugar, then pound to a paste. Squeeze in lime juice and stir in water and fish sauce until it is well mixed. Store in the refrigerator until ready to use, for a maximum of 2 weeks.

Makes about 1 cup

korean dipping sauce

see variations page 66

This vinegary dipping sauce enhances the taste of broiled foods or raw vegetables. It can also be used as a marinade for meat, poultry, or seafood to be broiled or as a dressing for salads. This sauce keeps well in the refrigerator.

1/2 cup Chinese white rice vinegar
1 oz. fresh gingerroot, peeled and grated
2 tbsp. soy sauce
2 tbsp. sugar

2 tsp. sesame oil
2 cloves garlic, peeled and crushed
2 scallion bulbs, trimmed and finely chopped
1 tsp. chili powder

In a bowl, whisk together rice vinegar, gingerroot, and soy sauce. Beat in sugar until it has dissolved. Stir in sesame oil, garlic, scallion, and chili powder, and put aside for 1–2 hours to allow flavors to mingle before serving.

Makes about 1 cup

japanese teriyaki sauce

see variations page 67

Perhaps the best-known Japanese sauce, teriyaki sauce is often served with chicken or fish. Traditionally it is brushed onto meat, chicken, or fish, just as it comes off the grill, but it can also be served as a dipping sauce.

1/2 cup mirin (sweetened rice wine)
2 tbsp. soy sauce

1 tbsp. tamari sauce
1/2 cup sake

Pour ingredients into a small pan and bring to a boil. Reduce heat and simmer gently for about 15 minutes, until the liquid has reduced a little. Brush onto cooked meat or fish, or serve hot as a dipping sauce.

Makes about 1 cup

variations

malaysian chile relish

see base recipe page 49

chile & gingerroot relish
Add 1 ounce fresh gingerroot, peeled and chopped. Grind to a paste with
roasted shrimp paste and chiles.

chile & lemongrass relish
Add 2 lemongrass stalks, trimmed and sliced. Grind to a paste with roasted
shrimp paste and chiles.

chile relish with cilantro
Omit lime leaves and follow basic recipe. Beat a small bunch of fresh cilantro
leaves, finely chopped, into paste and spoon it into a small bowl.

chile relish with roasted coriander & cumin
Omit lime leaves. Add 2 teaspoons coriander seeds and 1 teaspoon cumin
seeds, both roasted and ground, to basic recipe.

chile relish with mint
Omit lime leaves. Add 2 teaspoons dried mint to chile mixture.

chile & garlic relish with shallots
Omit shrimp paste and grind chiles with 2 cloves of garlic instead. Beat
2 shallots, very finely chopped, into paste at the end.

indonesian fiery peanut sauce

see base recipe page 50

thai peanut sauce
Omit tamarind paste, soy sauce, and chili powder. Stir in 1–2 tablespoons red Thai curry paste instead.

vietnamese peanut sauce
Omit shallot, shrimp paste, and sugar. Replace with an extra clove of garlic and 2 red chiles, seeded and finely chopped. Stir garlic and chiles in oil for 2 minutes before adding peanuts. Replace tamarind, soy sauce, chili powder, and water with 2 tablespoons each hoisin sauce and fish sauce and 1/2 cup each coconut milk and chicken stock. Beat in small bunch of finely chopped cilantro.

hot & sour peanut sauce with mint & lime
Add 2 red chiles, seeded and chopped, with shallot and garlic. Replace tamarind paste and chili powder with juice of 1 lime and finely chopped mint leaves.

hot & sour walnut sauce
Omit chili powder. Add 2 red chiles, seeded and chopped, with shallot and garlic. Replace peanuts with walnuts.

hot & sour almond sauce
Omit chili powder. Add 2 red chiles, seeded and chopped, with shallot and garlic. Replace peanuts with toasted almonds.

variations

filipino lime sauce

see base recipe page 53

filipino lime sauce with gingerroot
Add 1 ounce fresh gingerroot, peeled and finely grated.

filipino lime sauce with chile
Add 1 finely chopped fresh chile, stalk and seeds removed.

cambodian lime sauce
Add 1 lemongrass stalk, trimmed and finely chopped; 1 red chile, seeded and
finely chopped; and a small bunch of fresh cilantro, finely chopped. Thin sauce
with a little water.

tamarind & lime sauce
Omit fish sauce and add 2 teaspoons tamarind paste and 2 chiles, seeded and
chopped, to lime juice. Thin with a little water.

filipino coconut vinegar & lime sauce
Replace 1 lime with 2–3 tablespoons coconut vinegar. Omit fish sauce and
add 2 red chiles, seeded and finely chopped; 2 cloves garlic, finely chopped;
and 2 scallions, trimmed and finely chopped.

sweet & sour coconut vinegar
Omit fish sauce. Combine 1–2 tablespoons coconut vinegar with juice of
1 lime. Stir in 1 tablespoon palm sugar until it dissolves.

variations

cambodian herbal paste

see base recipe page 54

indonesian herbal paste
Add 2–3 red chiles, seeded and finely chopped, and 2 teaspoons palm sugar to basic recipe. Grind to a paste with the other ingredients.

herbal paste with roasted coconut
In a heavy skillet, dry-roast 2 tablespoons fresh or dried unsweetened coconut, then add it to herbal paste. Dilute with a little water if too thick.

herbal paste with cilantro
Prepare basic recipe, adding a small bunch of fresh cilantro, finely chopped.

herbal paste with mint
Prepare basic recipe, adding a small bunch of fresh mint leaves, finely chopped.

herbal paste with basil
Prepare basic recipe, adding a small bunch of fresh basil leaves, finely shredded.

pungent herbal paste
Dry-roast 1 tablespoon shrimp paste with 2 teaspoons palm sugar in a heavy skillet. Add to the other ingredients and pound to a paste.

variations

vietnamese dipping sauce

see base recipe page 57

vietnamese dipping sauce with gingerroot
Prepare basic recipe, but add 1 ounce fresh gingerroot, peeled and chopped, to the garlic and chile, and use 1 whole lime.

vietnamese dipping sauce with soy
Replace water with 3–4 tablespoons soy sauce and reduce fish sauce to 2–3 tablespoons.

cambodian dipping sauce with lemongrass & cilantro
Add 2 lemongrass stalks, trimmed and chopped, and a small bunch of fresh cilantro, coarsely chopped, to garlic and chile, and use 2 whole limes.

spicy vinegar dipping sauce
Replace water and fish sauce with 4 tablespoons rice vinegar and 2 tablespoons soy sauce.

sweet & sour lime dipping sauce with mirin
Replace the half lime, water, and fish sauce with 1 tablespoon rice vinegar, 2 tablespoons soy sauce, juice of 2 limes, and 1/2 cup mirin (sweetened rice wine).

sweet & sour lime dipping sauce with gingerroot
Add 1 ounce gingerroot, peeled and chopped, to garlic and chile. Omit water and stir in juice of 2 limes and fish sauce.

variations

korean dipping sauce

see base recipe page 58

korean dipping sauce with roasted sesame seeds
Prepare basic recipe. Roast 2 tablespoons sesame seeds in a skillet until they emit a nutty aroma. Stir most of the seeds into sauce, then scatter the rest on top.

korean dipping sauce with lime
Prepare basic recipe, but replace garlic and scallion with zest and juice of 1 lime.

korean dipping sauce with mustard
Prepare basic recipe. Beat in 1–2 tablespoons Chinese hot mustard paste (available in Asian stores) or, alternatively, 1–2 tablespoons powdered mustard combined with a scant tablespoon of water.

korean dipping sauce with daikon
Prepare basic recipe, but replace scallion with 2 ounces fresh daikon, peeled and grated.

korean dipping sauce with chile
Prepare basic recipe, but omit chili powder and add 1–2 chiles, seeded and finely chopped.

korean dipping sauce with honey
Prepare basic recipe, but replace sugar with 2 tablespoons honey.

variations

japanese teriyaki sauce

see base recipe page 60

teriyaki sauce with garlic
Add 2 crushed garlic cloves after sauce has boiled.

teriyaki sauce with gingerroot
Add 1 ounce fresh gingerroot, peeled and grated, after sauce has boiled.

teriyaki sauce with chile & scallions
After sauce has boiled, add 1 red chile, stalk and seeds removed and finely chopped, and 2 scallions, trimmed to the white bulbs and finely chopped.

sweet teriyaki sauce
After sauce has boiled, lower heat and stir in 2 tablespoons rock or palm sugar until it dissolves.

dashi sauce
Mix basic teriyaki sauce with 2/3 cup dashi—a sea-flavored stock prepared from dried kelp (konbu) and dried fish flakes, or a brown fish stock (katsuo-bushi), available in some Asian markets. Serve with Japanese tempura.

dashi sauce with gingerroot & daikon
Prepare dashi sauce as above. Peel and grate 1 ounce gingerroot and 2 ounces daikon, and stir into sauce just before serving.

broths & soupy noodles

From palate cleansers to elaborate dishes, broths

and soups are fundamental to an Asian meal. Clear

and subtle or thick and complex, spanning the

spectrum of Asian flavorings, broths and soupy

noodles are often accompanied by colorful, crunchy

vegetables, herbs, and fresh chiles.

vietnamese winter melon broth with tiger lilies

see variations page 88

Appreciated for their beauty and subtle flavor, winter melon and tiger lilies are available in Asian markets. When choosing tiger lilies, make sure they are light golden in color.

for the stock

1 1/4 lbs. pork ribs

1 onion, peeled and quartered

2 medium-sized carrots, peeled and cut into chunks

1 oz. dried shrimp, soaked in water for 15 minutes, rinsed and drained

1 tbsp. fish sauce

1 tbsp. soy sauce

4 black peppercorns

sea salt

12 oz. winter melon

1 oz. tiger lilies

sea salt

freshly ground black pepper

small bunch fresh cilantro leaves, chopped

small bunch fresh mint leaves, chopped

To prepare stock, put ribs in large stockpot and cover with approximately 7 cups of water. Bring water to a boil, skim off any fat, and add remaining ingredients. Cover pot and simmer for 1 1/2 hours, then skim off any foam or fat, and continue to simmer stock, uncovered, for another 30 minutes. Strain stock and check seasoning. You should have roughly 5 cups. Store in refrigerator up to 3 days or in freezer until ready to use. Halve melon lengthwise. Remove seeds and inner membrane. Slice into thin half-moon slices. Soak tiger lilies in pan of hot water, covered, for about 20 minutes. Remove, squeeze dry, and tie in a knot. Bring stock to a boil in a deep pot or wok. Reduce heat and add winter melon and tiger lilies. Simmer for 15–20 minutes, until winter melon is tender. Season to taste, scatter cilantro and mint leaves over top, and serve immediately.

Serves 4

cambodian hot & sour fish soup

see variations page 89

Various versions of this tangy soup can be found throughout Southeast Asia, with the emphasis on hot, sweet, and sour varying from region to region. In Cambodia, chiles provide heat, tamarind produces tartness, and ripe pineapple adds a fruity, sweet note.

2 tbsp. fish sauce
juice of 2 limes
2 cloves garlic, finely chopped
freshly ground black pepper
1 fresh catfish, sea bass, or red snapper (about
    2 1/4 lbs.), filleted
1 tbsp. vegetable oil
2 scallions, trimmed and sliced
2 shallots, sliced
1 1/2 oz. fresh galangal, peeled and chopped
2 lemongrass stalks, cut into strips and crushed
1 oz. dried squid, soaked in water for 30
    minutes, rinsed, and drained

2 tbsp. tamarind paste
2–3 red Thai chiles, seeded and sliced
1 tbsp. palm sugar (or sugar of your choice)
2–3 tbsp. fish sauce
1/2 lb. fresh pineapple, peeled and diced
3 tomatoes, skinned, seeded, and chopped
2 oz. canned sliced bamboo shoots, drained
small bunch fresh cilantro, finely chopped
sea salt and freshly ground black pepper
1 lime, quartered
big handful of fresh bean sprouts
big bunch of feathery dill weed, chopped

Combine fish sauce, lime juice, garlic, and black pepper in a large bowl. Cut fish into bite-size pieces, reserving head, tail, and bones for stock. Put fish chunks in marinade, toss lightly, cover, and set aside. Heat oil in a deep pan and stir in scallions, shallots, galangal, lemongrass, and dried squid. Add fish head, bones, and tail, and sauté gently for a minute or two. Pour in roughly 4 cups water and bring to a boil. Reduce heat and simmer for 30 minutes. Strain stock into another deep pan, then bring clear stock to a boil. Stir in tamarind paste, chiles, sugar, and fish sauce, and simmer for 2–3 minutes. Add pineapple, tomatoes,

and bamboo shoots, and simmer for 2–3 minutes more. Finally stir in fish chunks with
cilantro and cook until fish turns opaque. Season to taste, then ladle soup into hot bowls.
Serve with lime quarters to squeeze over it, and garnish with bean sprouts and dill weed.

Serves 4

singapore laksa

see variations page 90

There are many different laksas, but all are based on noodles cooked in a spicy coconut broth. Rich and creamy, Singapore laksa marries the Malay and Chinese styles of cooking.

for the spice paste
8 shallots, peeled and chopped
4 cloves garlic, peeled and chopped
1 1/2 oz. fresh gingerroot, peeled and chopped
2 stalks lemongrass, trimmed and chopped
6 candlenuts (or macadamia nuts)
4 dried red chiles, soaked and seeded
2 tbsp. dried shrimp, soaked until soft
1–2 tsp. shrimp paste
1–2 tsp. palm sugar (or sugar of your choice)
1 tbsp. vegetable oil

4–6 shallots, peeled and finely sliced
2 1/2 cups unsweetened coconut milk
1 3/4 cup chicken stock
3 1/2 oz. fresh shrimp, shelled
3 1/2 oz. fresh squid, cleaned and sliced
6–8 fresh small scallops
3 oz. fresh clams, shelled
sea salt and freshly ground black pepper
1/2 lb. fresh rice noodles or dried rice vermicelli,
    soaked in lukewarm water until pliable
3 1/2 oz. fresh bean sprouts
small bunch fresh mint, roughly chopped
chili oil

Make spice paste, using a mortar and pestle or a blender to grind all the ingredients, except oil. Bind paste with 1 tablespoon oil and set aside. Heat enough oil in a wok to deep-fry shallots. Fry shallots until crisp and golden. Drain shallots onto a piece of paper towel and set aside. Discard the oil, reserving 2 tablespoons. Heat reserved oil in wok and stir in spice paste. Cook over low heat for 3–4 minutes, until fragrant. Add coconut milk and chicken stock. Bring to a boil, stirring all the time. Add shrimp, squid, scallops, and clams, and simmer gently just until cooked. Season with salt and pepper. To serve, divide noodles among individual bowls. Add bean sprouts and ladle broth and seafood over top, making sure noodles are submerged. Garnish with crispy shallots, mint, and a drizzle of chili oil.

Serves 4–6

chicken & gingerroot broth with papaya

see variations page 91

In the rural areas of the Philippines, this traditional peasant dish is still cooked daily. One of the most popular versions is this one, with green papaya in the broth, which is generally served with steamed rice or sipped throughout the meal to cleanse and stimulate the palate.

1–2 tbsp. palm or peanut oil
2 cloves garlic, finely chopped
1 large onion, halved and sliced
1 1/2 oz. fresh gingerroot, peeled and shredded
2 dried chiles, left whole
1 (2–3 lbs.) whole organic or corn-fed chicken, left whole or jointed, and trimmed of fat

2 1/2 cups chicken stock
4 cups water
2 tbsp. fish sauce
sea salt and freshly ground black pepper
1 small green papaya, cut into fine slices
bunch of fresh young chile leaves (or flat-leaf parsley leaves)

Heat oil in a wok or deep pot, and stir in garlic, onion, and gingerroot until they begin to color. Stir in chiles and add chicken to lightly brown the skin. Pour in stock, water, and fish sauce, making sure chicken is completely covered (add more water if necessary), and bring liquid to a boil. Reduce heat, cover wok or pot, and simmer gently for about 1 1/2 hours, until chicken is very tender. Season stock with salt and pepper and add sliced green papaya. Continue to simmer for 10–15 more minutes, then stir in chile or parsley leaves. Serve chicken with plain steamed rice and ladle broth over top.

Serves 4–6

indonesian pumpkin, snake bean & bamboo soup

see variations page 92

This tasty soupy stew is generally served on its own with rice, but because it is thick, it can also be served as an accompaniment to broiled fish and meat dishes. On its own, it is an extremely satisfying vegetarian meal.

for the spice paste
4 shallots, peeled and chopped
1 oz. gingerroot, peeled and chopped
4 fresh red chiles, seeded and chopped
2 cloves garlic, peeled and chopped
1 tsp. coriander seeds
4 roasted candlenuts (or macadamia nuts), chopped

2 tbsp. palm, peanut, or corn oil
scant 1/2 lb. fresh pumpkin flesh, chopped into bite-size cubes
1/4 lb. snake beans
4 oz. canned bamboo shoots, drained and rinsed
3 cups unsweetened coconut milk
2–3 tsp. palm sugar
salt to taste
1/4 lb. fresh coconut, shredded

To make spice paste, use a mortar and pestle to grind ingredients together, or whiz them in an electric blender. Heat oil in a wok or heavy pan, and stir in spice paste until fragrant. Toss pumpkin, snake beans, and bamboo shoots in paste and pour in coconut milk. Add sugar and bring liquid to a boil. Reduce heat and cook gently for 10–15 minutes, until vegetables are tender. Season soup with salt and stir in half the fresh coconut. Spoon soup into bowls, sprinkle with remaining coconut, and serve with Malaysian chile relish (page 49) or Filipino lime sauce (page 53).

Serves 4

vietnamese beef noodle soup

see variations page 93

Some would say that this traditional soup, pho, is Vietnam in a bowl. It is Vietnamese fast-food for the working man as well as family food—everyman's dish of yin and yang —indulged in with joy and gusto at any time of day or night.

for the stock
3 1/2 lbs. oxtail, trimmed of fat and cut into thick pieces
2 1/4 lbs. beef shanks or brisket
2 large onions, peeled and quartered
2–3 carrots, peeled and cut into chunks
1 1/2 oz. fresh gingerroot, cut into chunks
6 cloves
2 cinnamon sticks
6 star anise
1 tsp. black peppercorns
2 tbsp. soy sauce
2–3 tbsp. fish sauce
sea salt

generous 1 lb. dried rice sticks, soaked in lukewarm water for 20 minutes, drained and set aside
generous 1/2 lb. beef sirloin, cut against grain into very thin pieces (size of heel of a hand)
1 onion, halved and finely sliced
6–8 scallions, trimmed, and cut into long pieces
2–3 fresh red chiles, seeds removed and finely sliced
4 oz. fresh bean sprouts
big bunch of fresh cilantro leaves, roughly chopped
big bunch of fresh mint leaves, roughly chopped
2 limes, quartered, for serving
hoisin sauce, for serving

To make stock, put oxtail into a large, deep pot and cover with water. Bring to a boil and blanch meat for 10–15 minutes. Drain meat, rinse off any scum, and clean pot. Put oxtail back into pot with other stock ingredients, apart from the fish sauce and salt, and cover with roughly 10–11 cups of water. Bring to a boil, reduce heat, and simmer, covered, for 2–3 hours. Remove lid and simmer for another hour, until stock has reduced to about 7 cups. Skim off any fat and strain stock into another pot.

Bring stock to a boil once more, stir in fish sauce, season to taste with salt, then reduce heat and leave stock simmering gently until ready to use.

Meanwhile, bring a pot filled with water to a boil, toss in noodles, and cook until tender—you may need to separate them with chopsticks if they stick together. Drain noodles and divide among 6 wide soup bowls. Top each serving with slices of beef, onions, scallions, and chiles. Ladle hot stock over the top, garnish with bean sprouts and fresh herbs, and serve with lime wedges to squeeze into soup and hoisin sauce to add sweetness.

Serves 4

chinese wonton soup

see variations page 94

Wontons are small, delicate dumplings filled with a pork and shrimp mixture. They can be deep-fried and served as a snack, or poached in a fragrant broth and served with rice or noodles. Wonton wrappers are available in Asian markets.

for the filling
6 oz. lean pork, finely ground
1/4 lb. fresh shelled shrimp, ground
1 tsp. granulated sugar
1 tsp. sesame oil
1 tbsp. rice wine
1 tbsp. soy sauce
2 scallions, trimmed and finely chopped
1/2 oz. fresh gingerroot, peeled and grated

24 wonton wrappers
3 cups chicken stock
1 tbsp. soy sauce
sea salt and freshly ground black pepper
2 scallions, trimmed and finely sliced

Combine filling ingredients in a bowl and, using your hands, knead mixture until smooth and pasty. Let stand for about 30 minutes. Place wonton wrappers under a damp cloth or plastic wrap to keep them from drying out as you work. Place one wrapper on a lightly floured surface and put a heaped teaspoon of filling in the center. Using your fingers, wet edges of wrapper with a little water and then press them together to seal—it should be plump in the middle with pointy ends. Place completed wonton under damp cloth and repeat with the rest. Bring stock to a boil and drop in wontons, one by one, so they don't stick together. Reduce heat and simmer for about 10 minutes. Stir in soy sauce and season stock with a little salt and pepper. Garnish with scallions and serve immediately.

Serves 4

japanese miso soup with tofu

see variations page 95

This soup is prepared with white miso, a pungent paste made from soybeans and yellow in color. (There is also a saltier version, which is reddish-brown.) Traditionally, miso soups use dashi, a stock made from kelp and dried fish flakes. Both miso and dashi are available in Asian markets.

4 cups dashi (homemade or instant)
1/2 lb. tofu, diced

2 tbsp. white miso paste
2 scallions, trimmed and finely sliced

Reserve roughly 1/2 cup dashi and pour the rest into a pot. Bring to a boil, reduce heat, and add tofu. Stir for 2–3 minutes. In a bowl, beat miso with reserved dashi until smooth, then stir into soup. Simmer for 2–3 minutes until soup is thoroughly combined, then stir in most of the scallions. Ladle soup into bowls and garnish with remaining scallions.

Serves 4

thai spicy shrimp soup

see variations page 96

Packed with lemongrass, galangal, kaffir lime leaves, chile, basil, and tamarind, this popular soup conjures up the flavors of Southeast Asian cooking. Traditionally served with jasmine rice, it also suffices as a delicious meal on its own.

for the marinade
4 cups fish or shellfish stock
2 tbsp. fish sauce
1 tbsp. tamarind paste
2 cloves garlic, crushed
1 1/2 oz. fresh galangal, peeled and finely sliced
2 stalks lemongrass, trimmed and finely sliced

3–4 fresh red chiles, left whole
4 kaffir lime leaves, lightly crushed with your fingers
20 medium shrimp, shelled and deveined
sea salt to taste
small bunch Thai basil leaves, shredded

Bring stock to a boil in a deep pot. Stir in fish sauce, tamarind paste, garlic, galangal, lemongrass, chiles, and kaffir lime leaves. Reduce heat and simmer for about 30 minutes to flavor stock.

Add shrimp and simmer for 2–3 minutes until cooked through. Season soup with salt to taste and stir in half the basil. Ladle soup into bowls and garnish with remaining basil.

Serves 4

korean pickled cabbage soup

see variations page 97

This unique pickled cabbage, kimchi, is served as an accompaniment to almost any dish in Korea, and it is also a popular snack. Some cooks combine the pickling liquid with water and heat it up as the stock for this soup. You can find jars of kimchi at Asian markets.

4 cups chicken stock
8 oz. drained kimchi, cut into bite-size pieces
1 oz. fresh gingerroot, finely sliced

2 tbsp. soy sauce
sea salt and freshly ground black pepper

Bring stock to a boil in a deep pot. Stir in kimchi and ginger with soy sauce. Reduce heat and simmer for about 30 minutes. Season stock with salt and pepper and ladle it into bowls. Serve soup on its own or with steamed rice.

Serves 4

vietnamese winter melon broth with tiger lilies

see base recipe page 69

winter melon broth with gingerroot & lemongrass
Replace tiger lilies with 1 ounce gingerroot, peeled and finely sliced, and
2 lemongrass stalks, peeled, trimmed, and finely sliced.

winter melon broth with lotus root & basil
Replace tiger lilies with 1/2 pound fresh lotus root, peeled and finely sliced.
Add it to stock 10 minutes before the winter melon. Garnish broth with small
fresh basil leaves instead of mint and cilantro.

winter melon broth with green papaya & cilantro
Replace tiger lilies with 1/2 pound green papaya, peeled and finely sliced, to
give a tart flavor to broth. Omit fresh mint; garnish only with fresh cilantro,
finely chopped.

winter melon broth with green mango
Replace tiger lilies with 1/2 pound green mango, peeled, pitted, and finely sliced.
Omit fresh mint; garnish only with fresh cilantro, finely chopped.

winter melon broth with shiitake mushrooms
Replace tiger lilies with 1/4 pound dried shiitake mushrooms, soaked in water
for 20 minutes. Squeeze mushrooms dry, discard stems, slice caps into strips,
and add to broth with winter melon.

cambodian hot & sour fish soup

see base recipe page 70

hot & sour fish soup with mango

Replace pineapple and bamboo shoots with 1 large, ripe, but firm mango, peeled and finely sliced. Add mango to clear broth with tamarind paste and chiles and proceed with basic recipe.

hot & sour shrimp soup

Replace fish with 2 pounds shrimp. Shell shrimp and toss them in marinade. Add shells to stock. Proceed with basic recipe.

hot & sour pork soup

Replace fish with 1 1/4 pounds boneless pork, cut into thin strips. Marinate and proceed with basic recipe.

hot & sour chicken soup

Replace fish with 1 1/4 pounds chicken breast, cut into thin strips. Marinate strips and proceed with basic recipe.

hot & sour tofu soup

Replace fish with 9 ounces tofu, rinsed and drained. Cut tofu into bite-size cubes, and toss in marinade (if vegetarian, substitute soy sauce for fish sauce). Add tofu to soup with tamarind paste.

variations

singapore laksa

see base recipe page 73

singapore laksa with snake beans & bamboo shoots
Omit fried shallots, clams, and bean sprouts. Add 6 ounces bite-size snake beans
and 4 ounces bamboo shoots to wok for 6–8 minutes before shellfish.

vegetarian laksa
Omit dried shrimp and shrimp paste from spice paste. Replace chicken stock
with vegetable stock flavored with 2–3 tablespoons soy sauce. Replace shellfish
with bite-size snake beans, bamboo shoots, and quartered tomatoes.

laksa with chicken
Omit scallops and clams. Toss 2 chicken breasts, finely sliced, in spice paste
before adding coconut milk and chicken stock.

laksa with tofu & shiitake mushrooms
Replace scallops with 8 ounces cubed tofu. Replace clams with 4 1/2 ounces
dried shiitake mushrooms (soaked 20 minutes, squeezed dry, and quartered).

laksa with toasted coconut & pineapple
Omit deep-fried shallots. Garnish with cilantro instead of mint, 2–3 tablespoons
roasted coconut, and 2–3 slices fresh pineapple (in thin chunks). Drizzle with
chili oil and sweet soy sauce.

chicken & gingerroot broth with papaya

see base recipe page 74

tofu & gingerroot broth with papaya
Replace chicken with 1 pound cubed tofu, and reduce cooking liquid to 4 cups
chicken stock only. Simmer stock just 25–30 minutes, season to taste, stir in
papaya and chile leaves together, and serve.

pork & gingerroot broth with papaya
Replace chicken with generous 1 pound lean pork, in thin strips. Stir pork with
chiles in wok, then add fish sauce with 4 cups chicken or pork stock only.
Reduce simmering time to 40 minutes.

shrimp & gingerroot broth with papaya
Omit chicken. Proceed with basic recipe and bring 4 cups chicken stock to a boil.
Simmer for 40 minutes, then add papaya for 5 minutes before adding 9 ounces
shelled shrimp to cook 5–10 minutes.

chicken & lemongrass broth with green mango
Add 4 lemongrass stalks, trimmed, quartered, and bruised, to oil with the chiles.
Replace green papaya with green mango, finely diced or shredded.

vegetarian gingerroot broth with papaya
Replace chicken stock with vegetable stock and fish sauce with soy sauce.

indonesian pumpkin, snake bean & bamboo soup

see base recipe page 77

cambodian spinach, snake bean & bamboo soup

Omit gingerroot and use 1 1/2 ounces each fresh galangal and turmeric, peeled and chopped. Omit pumpkin and double the beans. Simmer vegetables for 10 minutes, then add 6 ounces fresh spinach and simmer 5 more minutes.

filipino pork, snake bean & bamboo soup with lime

Double gingerroot and replace pumpkin with 6 ounces pork, in thin strips or cubes. Stir-fry pork in spice paste for 2–3 minutes before adding beans, bamboo shoots, coconut milk, and juice of 2 calamondin oranges.

tofu, snake bean & bamboo soup

Replace pumpkin with 6 ounces cubed tofu. Garnish with small bunch of finely chopped fresh cilantro and the coconut. Serve with wedges of lime to squeeze into soup.

butternut squash & snake bean soup

Replace pumpkin with 1/2 pound butternut squash. Omit bamboo shoots.

pumpkin, snake bean & shrimp soup

Replace bamboo shoots with 6 ounces shelled shrimp. Add 1–2 tablespoons fish sauce and 1–2 tablespoons soy sauce to coconut milk.

variations

vietnamese beef noodle soup

see base recipe page 78

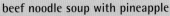

beef noodle soup with pineapple
Replace bean sprout garnish with fresh pineapple cubes. Drizzle with 1–2 tablespoons chili oil mixed with 1–2 tablespoons sweet soy sauce, omitting hoisin sauce and limes.

beef noodle soup with fresh coconut
Replace bean sprouts with grated flesh of half a coconut.

beef noodle soup with shrimp & cucumber
Cook 1/2 pound fresh, shelled shrimp in strained stock while preparing noodles. Replace bean sprouts with half a cucumber, peeled, seeded, and cut into matchsticks.

vietnamese chicken noodle soup
Replace oxtail and beef shank with a whole, free-range chicken. Simmer stock for about 1 1/2 hours. Tear cooked chicken into thick strips to use instead of beef.

vegetarian tofu noodle soup
Omit oxtail, beef shank, and fish sauce from stock and make a vegetable stock with remaining ingredients. Rinse a 9-ounce block of tofu, pat dry, and cut into thirds. Heat oil for deep-frying and slip in tofu. Fry until golden brown, drain, and finely slice. Substitute sliced tofu for sliced beef.

variations

chinese wonton soup

see base recipe page 81

wonton soup with tiger lilies
Soak 1 ounce tiger lilies in a covered pan of hot water for about 20 minutes. Squeeze dry, tie in a knot, and add to stock.

wonton soup with shiitake mushrooms
Soak 4 ounces dried shiitake mushrooms in warm water for 20 minutes. Squeeze dry, trim, and cut in half lengthwise. Add to stock.

wonton soup with gingerroot
Add 1 1/2 ounce gingerroot, peeled and finely sliced, to stock.

wonton soup with lemongrass & cilantro
Add 2 lemongrass stalks, halved and bruised, and a bunch of cilantro to stock.

wonton soup with noodles
When you drop wontons into stock, drop 6 ounces thin fresh egg noodles into a pot of boiling water and cook for about 3 minutes. Drain noodles and divide them among serving bowls. Ladle wonton soup over and serve immediately.

vegetarian wonton soup
Replace pork and shrimp in wonton filling with 1/2 pound tofu, rinsed and finely diced. Replace chicken stock with vegetarian stock.

variations

japanese miso soup with tofu

see base recipe page 82

japanese miso soup with wakame
Replace tofu with 3 1/2 ounces wakame sea vegetable (seaweed), soaked in water for 30 minutes and drained.

japanese miso soup with shiitake mushrooms
Replace tofu with 4 1/2 ounces dried shiitake mushrooms, soaked in water for 20 minutes, drained, trimmed, and cut into quarters.

japanese miso soup with string beans
Replace tofu with string beans, trimmed and cut into bite-size pieces. The beans will need to be simmered in the soup for 10 minutes to soften.

korean soybean soup with sesame oil
Replace miso with Korean soybean paste, toenjang, which is tan-colored and pungent. Ladle soup into bowls and drizzle with dark sesame oil.

korean soybean soup with chili oil
Replace sesame oil with chili oil. Garnish with a small bunch of fresh cilantro, finely chopped.

japanese red soybean soup with scallions
Replace white miso with red soybean paste. Omit tofu and stir in 4–6 scallions, trimmed and finely sliced, just before serving.

variations

thai spicy shrimp soup

see base recipe page 85

thai shrimp soup with tomatoes & cilantro
Add 1/2 pound cherry tomatoes to stock about 5 minutes before adding shrimp. Replace basil with a small bunch of fresh cilantro, roughly chopped.

spicy shrimp soup with bean sprouts
Prepare basic recipe. Divide 6 ounces fresh bean sprouts among individual bowls and ladle soup over them.

spicy shrimp soup with pineapple
Add 1/2 pound fresh pineapple, peeled, cored, and diced, to stock about 5 minutes before adding shrimp.

spicy shrimp & lime soup
Omit kaffir lime leaves. Serve with 2 fresh limes, cut into quarters, to squeeze into soup.

spicy shrimp & scallop soup
Add 1/2 pound small fresh scallops to stock just before adding shrimp.

spicy shrimp soup with pork
Add 6 ounces pork fillet, cut into thin strips, to stock about 10 minutes before adding shrimp.

korean pickled cabbage soup

see base recipe page 86

korean pickled cabbage soup with tofu
After stock has simmered, stir in 8 ounces cubed tofu. Simmer 5 minutes and serve.

pickled cabbage soup with noodles
Boil 8 ounces dried egg or wheat noodles in pot of water for 2 minutes, drain, put into individual bowls, add soup, and serve.

pickled cabbage soup with chicken & lemon
Add 2 chicken breasts to stock before simmering. After 30 minutes, shred chicken and divide into individual bowls. Ladle soup over and serve with lemon wedges.

pickled cabbage soup with fish & cilantro
After soup simmers 30 minutes, add 4 boned fish fillets and simmer 4–5 minutes, until just cooked. Divide fish among bowls, ladle soup over top, and garnish with chopped cilantro.

pickled cabbage soup with beef & scallions
After soup simmers 30 minutes, add 6 ounces beef fillet and simmer 8–10 minutes. Remove beef, slice finely, and divide among individual bowls. Ladle soup over sliced beef and scatter 2 scallions, finely sliced, over top.

rice, stir-fried noodles & spring rolls

Appearing on the table as steamed or stir-fried

grains, or ground into flour to make noodles,

dumplings, bread, and spring rolls, rice plays a

significant role in the Asian diet. Noodles in other

forms—wheat or egg—are also popular varieties.

asian sticky rice

see variations page 118

Sticky rice (also called glutinous rice) requires a long soaking in water before being cooked in a bamboo steamer. It is eaten on its own with dipping sauces, or it is served to accompany light dishes and vegetarian meals. Sticky rice grains are available in Asian markets and some supermarkets.

3/4 lb. white sticky rice
a bamboo steamer
a piece of cheesecloth

Put rice into a big bowl and fill bowl with water. Let soak for at least 6 hours. Drain, then rinse and drain again. Fill a wok or a heavy pan with enough water to come a third of the way up the sides. Place a bamboo steamer, with lid on, over wok and bring water to a boil. Lift off lid of steamer and place a dampened piece of cheesecloth over rack. Tip rice into the middle and spread it out a little. Fold edges of cheesecloth over rice, put lid back on steamer, and steam for about 25 minutes, until rice is tender but still firm.

Serves 4

malaysian coconut rice with turmeric

see variations page 119

Colored yellow by vibrant turmeric powder, this Malaysian rice is often served at festivals and at Malay and Indonesian food stalls. Regular, long-, or short-grain rice can be used for this dish, which is made by the traditional absorption method.

2–3 tbsp. vegetable or sesame oil
2–3 shallots, peeled and finely chopped
2 cloves garlic, peeled and finely chopped
1 lb. white long-grain rice, washed in several
    changes of water, and drained
1 (14-oz.) can unsweetened coconut milk
2 cups water

2 tsp. ground turmeric
3–4 fresh curry leaves
1/2 teaspoon salt and freshly ground black
    pepper
2 fresh red chiles, stalks and seeds removed,
    and finely sliced

Heat oil in a heavy pan and stir in shallots and garlic. Just as they begin to color, stir in rice until coated in oil. Add coconut milk, water, turmeric, curry leaves, salt, and pepper. Bring liquid to a boil, then turn down heat and put lid on pan. Cook gently for 15–20 minutes, until all liquid has been absorbed.

Turn off heat and let rice steam in pan for 10 minutes. Fluff up rice with a fork and garnish with sliced red chiles before serving.

Serves 4

filipino fried rice with chorizo & eggs

see variations page 120

This classic Filipino dish is often served for breakfast. It is a great way of using up leftover rice and is delicious served on its own or with meat and poultry dishes. If you don't have any leftover rice, cook 1/2 pound of rice the day before, using the absorption method, and refrigerate until ready to use. The Filipinos serve this rice with coconut vinegar; they dip spoonfuls or fingerfuls of the rice into small bowls of the vinegar.

1–2 tbsp. palm or peanut oil
2–3 cloves garlic, peeled and crushed
1 lb. cooked long-grain rice
1–2 tablespoons Filipino or Thai fish sauce
sea salt and freshly ground black pepper

for serving
2 whole chorizo sausages, sliced diagonally
2–3 tbsp. peanut or vegetable oil
4 eggs
4–6 tbsp. coconut vinegar

Heat oil in a wok or a heavy pan, stir in garlic, and cook until fragrant and golden. Toss in rice, breaking up any lumps, and add fish sauce. Season with salt, if needed, and black pepper, then turn off heat and cover pan with a lid to keep rice warm.

In a heavy pan, fry sliced chorizo in a tablespoon of oil until crispy on both sides. Drain chorizo on paper towel. Heat remaining oil in a separate pan and fry eggs sunny-side up or over-easy, making sure yolk remains soft and runny. Serve onto individual plates, place egg on top, and arrange chorizo around edge. Serve warm with coconut vinegar.

Serves 4

indonesian fried rice with sweet soy sauce

see variations page 121

This dish of fried rice is one of Indonesia's national dishes, and can be cooked at makeshift street stalls or top-class restaurants. It is generally made with leftover cooked grains. The fried rice is packed into a bowl, which is then inverted on a plate to form a mound. The rice is then crowned with a fried egg and served with thick, sweet Indonesian soy sauce.

2–3 tbsp. vegetable or peanut oil
4 shallots, finely chopped
4 cloves garlic, finely chopped
3–4 fresh red chiles, stalks and seeds removed, and chopped
3 tbsp. Indonesian sweet soy sauce

1 tbsp. tomato paste
3/4 lb. cooked long-grain rice
4 eggs
1/2 cucumber, peeled, halved lengthwise, seeds removed, and cut into thin sticks

In a wok, heat oil. Stir in shallots, garlic, and chiles until they begin to color. Add sweet soy sauce and tomato paste and stir for 2 minutes until thick and saucy. Toss in cooked rice and cook for about 5 minutes until well-flavored and heated through. In a shallow pan, heat a little oil for frying, then crack eggs into it. Fry until whites are cooked but yolks are runny. Divide the rice into 4 portions, then pack 1 portion into a deep bowl. Invert bowl onto an individual plate and then lift it off to reveal the mound of rice. Place an egg on top of mound and garnish with several cucumber sticks. Repeat with other 3 servings.

Serves 4

japanese rice porridge with green tea

see variations page 122

Rice porridge is popular throughout Asia, where it is often served for breakfast or as a snack. The basic porridge is generally served with leftover dishes or with family favorites such as salted or pickled fish and spicy sausages.

7 cups water
3–4 tbsp. green tea leaves
1/2 lb. short-grain rice

1–2 tbsp. sesame oil
soy sauce

Bring water to a boil in a large pot. Stir in green tea leaves, turn off heat, and let them steep for about 5 minutes. Strain tea into another pot, discard leaves, and bring it to a boil. Toss rice (don't rinse the rice grains—you need the starch to give porridge the required texture) into boiling tea, reduce heat to low, cover pot, and simmer for about 1 1/2 hours, until grains break down and have a porridge-like consistency.

Spoon porridge into individual bowls. Drizzle sesame oil over porridge and pass around soy sauce to splash over top.

Serves 4–6

thai stir-fried rice noodles

see variations page 123

This is the classic stir-fried noodle dish sold everywhere in Thailand by street hawkers and in cafes and restaurants. Dried shrimp are available in Asian markets.

1/2 lb. small dried rice sticks, or any dried
   noodles of your choice
2 tbsp. fish sauce
2 tbsp. palm or granulated sugar
2–3 tsp. tamarind paste
2 tbsp. sesame, peanut, or coconut oil
2 cloves garlic, peeled and crushed
4 1/2 oz. dried shrimp

8 oz. tofu, rinsed, drained, and sliced into thin
   strips
1 1/4 cups chicken or vegetable stock
2 eggs
2 scallions, trimmed, cut into bite-size pieces,
   and cut into strips
6 oz. bean sprouts, rinsed and drained
2 limes, cut into wedges

Put dried noodles in a bowl and cover with lukewarm water. Let stand for about 30 minutes until softened and pliable. Drain and set aside. In a small bowl, whisk together fish sauce, sugar, and tamarind paste until sugar has dissolved. Put aside. Heat half the oil in a wok, add garlic, and stir until fragrant. Add dried shrimp and tofu and stir-fry until garlic begins to brown. Toss in noodles and pour in stock. Stir until noodles have absorbed all the liquid. Stir in tamarind and fish sauce mixture and continue to stir-fry until noodles begin to crisp. Heat remaining oil in a skillet and crack eggs into it. Using a spatula or wooden spoon, mix yolks with whites as they cook, creating a flat egg that is partly white, partly yellow, and partly mixed together. Once eggs are firm, lift them out of oil onto a board and slice finely. Divide noodles among individual bowls and garnish each with sliced egg, shredded scallions, and bean sprouts. Serve with wedges of lime.

Serves 2–3

singapore stir-fried egg noodles

see variations page 124

This is a very popular stir-fried dish in Singapore, particularly with the Chinese population. Served at Malay, Indian, and Chinese hawker stalls, the dish is packed with ingredients and suffices as a meal on its own.

2–3 tbsp. vegetable oil
3 cloves garlic, peeled and finely chopped
1/4 lb. pork fillet, cut into thin strips
1/2 lb. fresh fish fillets (such as red snapper, grouper, trout), cut into bite-size pieces
1/4 lb. fresh shrimp, shelled and deveined
2 small squid, with innards and backbone removed, cleaned, and sliced (keep tentacles)

1 1/4 cups chicken stock
1 lb. fresh egg noodles
6 long white Chinese cabbage leaves, shredded
1 carrot, peeled and shredded
4 tbsp. soy sauce
freshly ground black pepper
small bunch fresh cilantro, roughly chopped

Heat oil in a wok and stir in garlic. When it becomes fragrant, stir in pork, fish, shrimp, and squid, tossing them around pan for a minute. Pour in stock and bring it to a boil to reduce. Add noodles and toss them around wok for a minute. Stir in shredded cabbage and carrot and add soy sauce—there should be very little liquid at this stage. Season with pepper, sprinkle with cilantro, and divide noodles among 4 bowls.

Serves 4

japanese soba noodles with shiitake mushrooms

see variations page 125

Japanese soba noodles are made from buckwheat and can be bought dried or frozen in Asian markets. This recipe can be prepared with fresh or dried shiitake mushrooms.

1/2 lb. dried soba noodles
3 tbsp. soy sauce
2 tbsp. mirin
2 tbsp. sake
1 tbsp. palm or granulated sugar
1 tbsp. sesame oil

1/2 lb. fresh shiitake mushrooms, trimmed and cut into thin strips
2 scallions, trimmed and finely sliced
1 oz. fresh gingerroot, peeled and cut into fine strips

Bring a pot of water to a boil and drop in noodles. Cook for about 2–3 minutes, untangling them with chopsticks, until tender but retaining a bite. Drain and refresh under cold water.

In a bowl, whisk together soy sauce, mirin, sake, and sugar, until sugar has dissolved. Put aside. Heat oil in a wok, then toss in mushrooms and cook for 2 minutes. Toss in noodles and pour in soy sauce and mirin mixture. Stir-fry until noodles are thoroughly coated, then divide among individual bowls. Garnish with scallions and gingerroot.

Serves 4

vietnamese summer rolls with pumpkin & tofu

see variations page 126

This is one of the great Vietnamese "do-it-yourself" dishes. You place all the prepared ingredients on the table along with the rice wrappers for everyone to assemble their own rolls. The ingredients vary with the seasons, and different dipping sauces can be added.

2 tbsp. peanut or sesame oil
6 oz. tofu, rinsed and patted dry
4 shallots, halved and sliced
2 cloves garlic, finely chopped
3/4 lb. pumpkin, with seeds removed, peeled, and cut into strips
1 carrot, peeled and cut into strips
1 tbsp. soy sauce
1/2 cup water

salt
3–4 fresh green chiles, seeded and sliced
small head of crisp lettuce, washed and torn into strips
bunch of fresh basil leaves
1/4 lb. roasted peanuts, chopped
scant 1/2 cup hoisin sauce
roughly 20 dried rice wrappers
6 tbsp. Vietnamese dipping sauce (page 57)

Heat a heavy pan and smear with a smidgeon of oil. Place block of tofu in pan and sear on both sides. Transfer to a plate and cut into thin strips. Heat remaining oil in pan and stir in shallots and garlic. Toss in pumpkin and carrot, then pour in soy sauce and water. Add a little salt to taste and cook gently until vegetables have softened but still have a bite. Meanwhile, arrange tofu, chiles, lettuce, basil, peanuts, and hoisin sauce in their separate dishes and put them on table. Fill a bowl with hot water and place it in center of table (or fill a small bowl for each person), and place stack of rice wrappers beside bowl. Tip cooked vegetables into a dish, and put on table.

To make rolls, each person takes a rice wrapper and dips it for a few seconds in water to soften. Then lay wrapper flat on table or on a plate, and just off center, spread a few strips of lettuce, followed by pumpkin mixture, some tofu, sprinkling of chiles, drizzle of hoisin sauce, basil, and peanuts, layering ingredients in a neat stack. Pull shorter edge (i.e., side with filling) up over stack, tuck in sides, and roll into tight cylinder. Dip roll into Vietnamese dipping sauce and take a bite.

Serves 4–5

chinese spring rolls with bean sprouts

see variations page 127

Traditionally spring rolls were prepared to celebrate the spring harvest and were, accordingly, packed with vegetables. Spring roll wrappers are available in Asian markets.

for dipping sauce
2 tbsp. black or rice vinegar
3 tbsp. soy sauce
1 tbsp. fresh gingerroot, grated

1–2 tbsp. sunflower or vegetable oil
1/2 lb. fresh bean sprouts, washed and drained
2 carrots, peeled and cut into fine matchsticks
4 1/2 oz. canned bamboo shoots, drained and cut into fine matchsticks

6 oz. fresh button or oyster mushrooms, cut into fine matchsticks
1 leek, trimmed and cut into fine matchsticks
1 tsp. salt
1–2 tsp. sugar
1–2 tbsp. soy sauce
freshly ground black pepper
20 spring roll wrappers
sunflower or vegetable oil for deep-frying

In a bowl, whisk together vinegar and soy sauce. Stir in gingerroot and let stand for 1–2 hours so flavors mingle. Heat oil in a wok and stir-fry all vegetables for about 2 minutes. Add salt, sugar, soy sauce, and pepper. Stir-fry for 1–2 minutes, until vegetables are tender but still retain a bite. Turn off heat and let vegetables cool. Place one wrapper on a flat surface and put roughly 2 spoonfuls of mixture down one side, about 2 inches from edge. Pull that edge over filling, tuck in ends, and roll wrapper into a tight log. Seal edges with a little water or mixture of cornstarch and water. Keep finished rolls under damp cloth or plastic wrap to prevent them from drying out. Heat enough oil in a wok for deep-frying. Fry rolls in batches for 2–3 minutes, until crispy and golden, then drain on paper towel. Serve hot with dipping sauce.

Serves 4

variations

asian sticky rice

see base recipe page 99

black sticky rice
Replace white sticky rice with black sticky rice grains.

sticky rice cakes with soy sauce
Cook rice. Let it cool, then roll small portions into bite-size balls. Serve as snack with soy sauce.

sticky rice cakes with vietnamese dipping sauce & chiles
Prepare sticky rice cakes as above. Serve with Vietnamese dipping sauce (page 57) and strips of fresh green chiles.

coconut sticky rice
In heavy pot, bring to boil 14 fluid ounces unsweetened coconut milk and 1 cup chicken stock or water. Stir in 1/2 pound sticky rice grains, soaked and drained. Stir once with a pinch of salt and simmer about 25 minutes, until liquid is absorbed. Turn off heat and let steam, covered, 10 minutes.

aromatic sticky rice porridge
In heavy pan, bring 4 cups water to boil. Stir in 1 ounce peeled and sliced gingerroot, 1 cinnamon stick, and 1/2 teaspoon salt. Add 1/2 pound sticky rice grains, soaked and drained, and simmer about 45 minutes, until thick. Serve for breakfast with fried fish or leftover broiled meat.

malaysian coconut rice with turmeric

see base recipe page 100

coconut rice with turmeric & chili
Stir onion and garlic with 1 teaspoon sugar until they begin to caramelize.
Add 1–2 teaspoons chili powder with turmeric. Omit curry leaves.

coconut rice with roasted cumin & coriander
Dry-roast 1 teaspoon each cumin and coriander seeds in heavy skillet
until they emit a nutty aroma. Grind to a powder and add to rice with the
ground turmeric.

coconut rice with gingerroot
Add 1 ounce fresh gingerroot, peeled and finely chopped, to onion and
garlic. Omit turmeric and curry leaves.

coconut rice with roasted coconut
Dry-roast 6 ounces dried shredded coconut, until golden brown. Add to rice
just before serving. Omit chiles.

coconut rice with cilantro & mint
Finely chop a small bunch of fresh cilantro and a small bunch of fresh mint
and toss into the rice just before serving.

variations

filipino fried rice with chorizo & eggs

see base recipe page 103

fried rice with shrimp & eggs
Replace chorizo with 1/2 pound shelled shrimp, sautéed in 1–2 tablespoons peanut oil until opaque.

fried rice with pork, eggs & malaysian chile relish
Replace chorizo with shredded leftover roast or broiled pork. Serve with Malaysian chile relish (page 49).

fried rice with fried fish & scallions
Omit chorizo and eggs and fry 4–8 small whole fish, such as sardines, in the oil instead. Or use leftover broiled or baked fish, flaked or in chunks. Put fish over rice and scatter 2 scallions, trimmed and finely sliced, on top. Serve with Malaysian chile relish (page 49) or coconut vinegar.

fried rice with bacon, eggs & onion
Replace chorizo with 6 bacon slices and 1 finely sliced onion, sautéed in 1–2 tablespoons peanut oil, until onions are golden brown and bacon is crisp.

vegetarian fried rice with eggs, gingerroot & lemongrass
Omit fish sauce from rice. Add 1 ounce gingerroot, peeled and finely chopped, and 2 lemongrass stalks, trimmed and finely sliced, to oil. Omit chorizo.

variations

indonesian fried rice with sweet soy sauce

see base recipe page 104

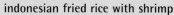

indonesian fried rice with shrimp
Add 1/2 pound fresh shelled shrimp to oil once shallots and garlic begin to color. Toss in rice for 1–2 minutes to heat through.

indonesian fried rice with tofu
Rinse and drain 8 ounces tofu and cut into small cubes. Toss in wok when shallots and garlic begin to color.

indonesian fried rice with pickled vegetables
Peel and slice 1 carrot, 1 daikon, and 1/2 cucumber into matchsticks. Toss with 3–4 tablespoons rice or coconut vinegar, 2 teaspoons sugar, and 1 teaspoon salt. Cover and marinate 2 hours before serving with rice.

malaysian fried rice with anchovy sauce & bean sprouts
Replace tomato paste with 1 tablespoon anchovy sauce. Omit eggs and cucumber. Stir-fry 1/2 pound fresh bean sprouts in a little oil and spoon over rice.

vietnamese fried rice with cucumber & green chiles
Replace sweet soy sauce with ordinary soy sauce. Omit tomato paste and eggs. Serve rice with cucumber sticks and 4 green chiles, seeded and sliced lengthwise.

variations

japanese rice porridge with green tea

see base recipe page 107

japanese green tea porridge with pickled ginger
Omit sesame oil. Serve with sliced pickled ginger.

chinese rice porridge with mushrooms & oyster sauce
Omit green tea. Sauté 1/2 pound oyster mushrooms, quartered, in
1–2 tablespoons peanut or sesame oil. Tip mushrooms over rice and
serve with commercial oyster sauce.

korean golden rice porridge with toasted sesame seeds
Omit green tea. Prepare rice with a fingerful of saffron fronds. Dry-roast
2 tablespoons sesame seeds to sprinkle over rice.

filipino rice porridge with chorizo, scallions & coconut vinegar
Omit green tea. Sauté 1–2 chorizo sausages, finely sliced, in 1–2 tablespoons
peanut oil, then spoon over rice. Scatter 2–3 scallions, finely sliced, over top
and splash with 1–2 tablespoons coconut vinegar.

vietnamese rice porridge with fish & chile dipping sauce
Omit green tea. Fry or steam 4 fresh fish fillets and place on top of rice.
Serve with Vietnamese dipping sauce (page 57).

variations

thai stir-fried rice noodles

see base recipe page 108

thai stir-fried rice noodles with fresh shrimp
Blanch 1/2 pound shelled fresh shrimp. Add shrimp to noodles with fish sauce mixture. Omit bean sprouts. Add chopped fresh cilantro to garnish.

thai stir-fried noodles with ketchup
Add 1–2 tablespoons ketchup to tamarind and fish sauce mixture. Omit sugar and bean sprouts.

chile stir-fried noodles
Add 2 fresh chiles, seeded and finely chopped, to garlic in wok. Add finely chopped cilantro to garnishes.

vegetarian stir-fried noodles
Omit dried shrimp. Replace chicken stock with vegetable stock. Add 1 ounce gingerroot, finely chopped, and 2 chiles, seeded and finely chopped, to garlic in wok.

stir-fried noodles with marinated tofu
Omit 8 ounces tofu, eggs, and bean sprouts from basic recipe. Cut 9 ounces of tofu into bite-size cubes. Whisk together 1 tablespoon sesame oil, 2 tablespoons soy sauce, 1 tablespoon honey, and 1 scant teaspoon chili powder, then marinate tofu for 30 minutes. Stir-fry marinated tofu in a little oil in a wok and spoon over cooked noodles.

variations

singapore stir-fried egg noodles

see base recipe page 111

stir-fried noodles with chicken & chorizo
Replace pork, fish, and shellfish with thin strips of 2 chicken breasts and 1 sliced chorizo sausage. Proceed with basic recipe.

stir-fried noodles with pork, shrimp & bean sprouts
Omit fish fillets, squid, and cabbage leaves. Increase amount of pork and shrimp to 1/2 pound each. Toss in 6 ounces fresh bean sprouts just before serving.

stir-fried noodles with shrimp, squid & scallops
Omit fish fillets, pork, and carrot. Add 1/4 pound shrimp and 1/2 pound scallops.

stir-fried noodles with pork, chicken & shiitake mushrooms
Replace fish and shellfish with thin strips of 2 chicken breasts. Add 1/2 pound shiitake mushrooms, soaked and trimmed, to stir-fried pork and chicken.

vegetarian stir-fried noodles with tofu
Replace pork, fish, shrimp, and squid with 12 ounces tofu, rinsed and cut bite-size. Replace chicken stock with vegetable stock and egg noodles with rice noodles.

variations

japanese soba noodles with shiitake mushrooms

see base recipe page 112

japanese soba noodles with bean sprouts
Replace mushrooms with bean sprouts, added just before serving.

japanese soba noodles with daikon
Replace mushrooms with 4 ounces daikon, peeled and cut into matchsticks.

japanese soba noodles with wasabi root
Omit mushrooms. Add 2 tablespoons finely grated wasabi root to soy sauce and mirin mixture.

japanese soba noodles with ginger & garlic
Omit mushrooms. Add 1 ounce fresh ginger, peeled and grated, and 2 cloves garlic, crushed, to oil in wok.

green tea soba noodles with chile
Omit mushrooms. Add 1 chile, seeded and finely chopped, to soy sauce and mirin mixture. Replace noodles with green tea soba noodles (called cha soba in Asian stores).

vietnamese summer rolls with pumpkin & tofu

see base recipe page 114

summer rolls with tofu & pickled vegetables
Omit pumpkin, carrot, shallot, and garlic. Peel and slice 2 carrots, 1 daikon, and 1 small cucumber into matchsticks. Toss with 3–4 tablespoons rice or coconut vinegar, 2 teaspoons sugar, and 1 teaspoon salt. Marinate 2 hours before filling wrappers.

summer rolls with butternut squash
Replace pumpkin and carrot with 1 pound butternut squash, peeled and cubed.

summer rolls with scallions & bean sprouts
Replace pumpkin and carrot with 6–8 scallions, bite-size, and 1/2 pound bean sprouts.

summer rolls with spicy shrimp & lime
Omit tofu, pumpkin, carrot, and water. Add 2 red or green chiles, finely chopped, to garlic and shallots, then add 9 ounces shelled shrimp until opaque. Add soy sauce. Serve with quartered limes.

rice wrappers with chicken & peanut sauce
Omit tofu, pumpkin, and carrot. Add 2–3 chicken breasts, cut into strips, and stir-fry with garlic and shallots. Toss in 2–3 tablespoons soy sauce. Serve with Indonesian fiery peanut sauce (page 50).

variations

chinese spring rolls with bean sprouts

see base recipe page 117

chinese spring rolls with pork
Thinly slice 1/2 pound pork fillet. Marinate in 1 tablespoon soy sauce mixed with 1 tablespoon rice vinegar and 2 teaspoons cornstarch for 30 minutes. Drain pork and add to wok just before vegetables. Proceed with basic recipe, adding marinade with soy sauce and sugar.

chinese spring rolls with shrimp
Heat oil in wok, add 2 finely chopped garlic cloves and 1/2 pound shelled and deveined small shrimp before adding vegetables.

filipino spring rolls with coconut vinegar
Heat oil in wok. Stir in 2 cloves garlic, finely chopped, and 1 ounce gingerroot, finely chopped. Add 1/2 pound finely sliced pork fillet and 6 ounces shelled and deveined small shrimp. Proceed with basic recipe, doubling amount of soy sauce. Serve with coconut vinegar for dipping.

vietnamese spring rolls with crabmeat
Soak 6 ounces cellophane noodles in hot water for 30 minutes until pliable and doubled. Drain and chop coarsely. Add noodles and 1/2 pound fresh or canned crabmeat to vegetables in wok. Add a little extra soy sauce, and serve with Vietnamese dipping sauce (page 57).

fish & shellfish

With 39,000 miles of coastline and many large rivers, Asia is blessed with a wide variety of saltwater and freshwater fish and shellfish. Synonymous with abundance and prosperity, fish and shellfish are cooked daily in soups, noodle and rice dishes, and stews.

indonesian fish & star fruit stew

see variations page 148

As is the nature of many Asian stews, this dish lies somewhere between a stew and a soup, ideal for serving with sticky rice or noodles. Choose small firm star fruit so that they retain a slight tartness.

for the spice paste
4 shallots, peeled and chopped
4 fresh red chiles, seeded and chopped
2 cloves garlic, chopped
1 oz. fresh galangal, peeled and chopped

1 oz. fresh turmeric, peeled and chopped
3–4 candlenuts (or macadamia nuts), chopped
2 tbsp. coconut or palm oil

2 lemongrass stalks, trimmed and bruised
1 oz. fresh gingerroot, finely sliced
roughly 1 1/2 lbs. freshwater or saltwater fish, such as trout or sea bream, cut into thin steaks
2 firm star fruit, sliced
juice of 1–2 limes
bunch of fresh basil leaves
1 lime, cut into wedges

Using a mortar and pestle, pound spice paste ingredients to form a coarse paste. Heat oil in a wide wok or heavy pan, then stir in spice paste until fragrant. Pour in roughly 3 cups water (enough to cover fish) and add lemongrass and gingerroot. Bring liquid to a boil, stirring all the time, then reduce heat and simmer for 10 minutes. Slip in fish steaks, making sure there is enough cooking liquid (add more water if necessary). Simmer gently for 3–4 minutes, then add star fruit and lime juice. Continue to simmer for another 2–3 minutes, until fish is cooked. Divide fish and star fruit between 4–6 bowls, spoon a little cooking liquid over the top, and garnish with basil leaves and a wedge of lime. Serve with bowls of steamed rice, moistened by spoonfuls of the remaining cooking liquid.

Serves 4–6

vietnamese fish steamed with beer

see variations page 149

This popular Vietnamese dish can be prepared with fish, shellfish, or both. In the Vietnamese markets, large crabs are sold specifically for this versatile dish, which can easily be adapted to feed as many people as you like.

2 whole firm-fleshed fish, weighing roughly
   1 lb. each, gutted and cleaned
salt and pepper
roughly 16 fl. oz beer
4 scallions, trimmed and chopped
1 oz. fresh gingerroot, peeled and finely sliced
2 fresh green or red chiles, stalk and seeds
   removed, and finely sliced

3 lemongrass stalks, finely sliced
bunch of fresh dill weed fronds, chopped
bunch of fresh basil leaves, chopped
bunch of fresh cilantro leaves, chopped
2 tbsp. fish sauce
juice of 1 lemon

Rub fish with salt and pepper and place it in basket of large steamer. Pour beer into base and scatter scallions, gingerroot, chiles, lemongrass, and herbs over fish. Steam for about 15 minutes, until the flesh is just cooked.

Lift fish onto serving dish and keep warm. Tip vegetables and herbs from steamer into beer and bring it to a boil for 2–3 minutes. Stir in fish sauce and lemon juice, season to taste, and pour into a bowl. Remove skin from fish and, using your fingers or a fork, tear off pieces of fish and dip them into flavored beer.

Serves 4

cambodian fish baked in coconut custard

see variations page 150

This is a classic Khmer dish that appears all over Cambodia. The fish, which is steamed in a custard made with coconut milk and flavored with the traditional Cambodian herbal paste, is delicious served with jasmine rice or fresh, crusty bread to mop up the sauce, and a salad.

2 (14-oz.) cans unsweetened coconut milk
3 large eggs
roughly 1/3 cup Cambodian herbal paste
    (page 54)
1 tbsp. fish sauce

2 tsp. palm sugar
2 1/4 lbs. skinless fresh white fish fillets, cut
    into 8 pieces
small bunch fresh cilantro, finely chopped

Preheat oven to 350°F.

In a bowl, beat coconut milk with eggs, herbal paste, fish sauce, and sugar, until well blended and sugar has dissolved. Place fish in an ovenproof dish and pour custard over it. Cover dish with aluminum foil and place in oven for 25–30 minutes.

Scatter cilantro over top and serve immediately with rice or chunks of fresh crusty bread.

Serves 4

saigon shrimp curry

see variations page 151

There are many variations of this delicious coconut milk-based curry all over Southeast Asia. Because there is a strong Indian influence in the culinary culture of southern Vietnam, this variation uses Indian curry powder.

1 oz. fresh gingerroot, roughly chopped
2–3 cloves garlic, roughly chopped
3 tbsp. peanut oil
1 onion, halved and finely sliced
2 stalks lemongrass, trimmed and finely sliced
2 fresh red or green chiles, stalk and seeds removed, and finely sliced
1 tbsp. sugar
2 tsp. shrimp paste

1 tbsp. fish sauce
2 tbsp. curry powder
2 generous cups canned unsweetened coconut milk
juice and zest of 1 lime
salt to taste
2 lbs. shrimp, shelled and deveined
small bunch basil leaves
small bunch cilantro leaves, finely chopped

Using a mortar and pestle, pound gingerroot with garlic until it almost resembles a paste. Heat oil in a traditional clay pot, wok, or heavy pot and stir in onion. Cook until it begins to turn brown, then stir in garlic-gingerroot paste. Once aromas begin to lift from pot, add lemongrass, chiles, and sugar. Cook for 1–2 minutes, before adding shrimp paste, fish sauce, and curry powder. Stir well and allow flavors to mingle and fuse over the heat for a minute or two, before adding coconut milk, lime juice, and zest. Mix well and bring liquid to a boil for 2–3 minutes. Season to taste with salt. Gently stir in shrimp and bring liquid to a boil once more. Reduce heat and cook gently for 2–3 minutes until shrimp turns opaque. Toss in basil leaves and sprinkle cilantro over top. Serve immediately from pot with chunks of crusty bread to mop up sauce.

Serves 4

malaysian grilled tamarind shrimp

see variations page 152

This is a great favorite from Malaysia. Rather expertly, the Malaysians crunch the whole shrimp, sucking in all the tamarind flavoring, while spitting out the bits of shell.

1 1/4 lbs. fresh large shrimp
2 tbsp. tamarind paste
2 tbsp. sweet soy sauce
1 tbsp. palm sugar

freshly ground black pepper
small bunch fresh cilantro, trimmed
2–4 fresh green chiles, stalks and seeds
    removed, quartered lengthwise

Devein shrimp, and trim feelers and legs, but keep shells on. Rinse well, pat dry, and, using a sharp knife, make an incision along the curve of the tail.

In a bowl, mix together tamarind paste, soy sauce, sugar, and black pepper. Pour mixture over shrimp, rubbing it over shells and into incision in tails. Cover and let marinate for 1 hour.

Prepare charcoal grill. Remove shrimp from marinade and place on rack over charcoal grill. Grill shrimp for about 3 minutes on each side, brushing them with marinade as they cook. Serve them immediately with cilantro leaves and chiles to chew on.

Serves 2–4

singapore chile crab

see variations page 153

Chile crab is an all-time favorite at hawker stalls and cafés in Singapore. To eat the crabs, crack the shells, then suck and dip the meat into the cooking sauce. Serve with crusty bread to mop up the sauce. Bowls are usually provided for the discarded pieces of shell and another with water for cleaning your fingers.

for the spice paste
4 cloves garlic, peeled and chopped
1 oz. fresh gingerroot, peeled and chopped
4 fresh red chiles, stalk and seeds removed, and chopped

vegetable oil for deep-frying
4 good-sized fresh crabs, cleaned, halved or quartered
2 tbsp. sesame oil

2–3 tbsp. chili sauce
3 tbsp. ketchup
1 tbsp. soy sauce
1 tbsp. palm sugar
1 cup chicken stock or water
salt and freshly ground black pepper
2 eggs, beaten
2 scallions, trimmed and finely sliced
small bunch fresh cilantro, finely sliced

Using a mortar and pestle or an electric blender, grind ingredients for spice paste and put aside. Heat enough oil for deep-frying in a wok or heavy pan. Drop in crabs and fry until shells turn bright red. Remove from oil and drain. Heat sesame oil in a separate wok and stir in spice paste. Fry until fragrant and stir in chili sauce, ketchup, soy sauce, and sugar. Toss in fried crab and coat well in sauce. Pour in chicken stock or water and bring liquid to a boil. Reduce heat and simmer for about 5 minutes. Season sauce to taste. Pour in beaten eggs, stirring gently, to let them set in the sauce. Serve immediately, garnished with scallions and cilantro.

Serves 4

filipino squid stuffed with ham & breadcrumbs

see variations page 154

This traditional Filipino dish of baby squid stuffed with a tasty mixture of breadcrumbs and Spanish ham reflects the Spanish influence in the nation's cuisine.

16 fresh baby squid
1–2 tbsp. palm or peanut oil
2–3 shallots, peeled and finely chopped
2–3 cloves garlic, finely chopped
4 oz. Serrano ham, finely chopped
1–2 tsp. paprika
small bunch flat-leaf parsley, finely chopped

6–8 slices white bread, crusts removed, ground to crumbs
1 1/4 cups dry white wine
1 1/4 cups chicken stock
2–3 bay leaves

First prepare squid: Use your fingers to pull off head and reach into body sac to pull out all innards and flat, thin bone. Rinse sac inside and out, and peel off skin. Cut tentacles above the eye, chop them finely, and put aside—discard everything else. Pat sacs dry before stuffing. Heat oil in heavy pan and stir in shallots and garlic until fragrant and beginning to color. Add Serrano ham and chopped squid tentacles, and fry for 2–3 minutes. Stir in paprika and chopped parsley and toss in breadcrumbs to absorb all juices and flavors—if it is a little dry, splash in 1–2 tablespoons of the wine. Set stuffing aside to cool. Stuff squid with breadcrumb filling and close each sac by threading a toothpick through the ends to prevent filling from spilling out. In a wide pan, bring wine and stock to a boil. Drop in bay leaves, reduce heat, and place stuffed squid in liquid. Cover pan and cook gently for 5–10 minutes. Transfer squid to serving dish. Spoon some of the cooking juices over them and garnish with a few parsley leaves.

Serves 6

chinese salt & pepper squid

see variations page 155

Life couldn't be simpler—squid fried with salt and pepper—a great Chinese tradition for all kinds of seafood. Ideal snack and finger food, the tender squid can be served on its own, with noodles, or with rice.

1 lb. baby or medium squid
2 tbsp. coarse salt
1 tbsp. freshly ground black pepper
2 tbsp. rice flour or cornstarch

vegetable or sesame oil for frying
1 green chile, sliced
2 limes, halved

Prepare squid by pulling head apart from body. Sever tentacles and trim. Reach inside body sac and pull out backbone, then clean it inside and out, removing any skin as well. Slice squid into rings, then pat them really dry. Place on a dish with tentacles. Mix salt and pepper with flour, tip it onto squid, and toss well, making sure it's fairly evenly coated.

Heat enough oil in a wok or heavy pan for deep-frying. Cook squid in batches, until rings turn crisp and golden. Drain on paper towel. Sprinkle with the chile, and serve with the lime to squeeze over it.

Serves 4

korean spicy fish braised with daikon

see variations page 156

In this traditional recipe the fish is braised until it practically falls apart, so you need to use a firm, fatty fish such as mackerel, sea bass, or trout.

generous 1/2 cup soy sauce
1–2 tbsp. sake
2–3 tbsp. palm sugar
2 tsp. sesame oil
1 1/2 oz. fresh gingerroot, peeled and grated
4 scallions, trimmed and finely sliced
4 cloves garlic, peeled and crushed

1 fresh red chile, seeded and finely chopped
1 lb. fresh daikon, peeled and thickly sliced
    (roughly 2/3 inch thick)
2 lbs. mackerel fillets, halved or cut into large
    chunks
2 cups fish stock
small bunch fresh cilantro, finely chopped

In a bowl, mix together soy sauce, sake, palm sugar, and sesame oil, until sugar has dissolved. Beat in gingerroot, scallions, garlic, and chile, and let stand for 30 minutes.

Place slices of daikon in a heavy-based pot. Place fish fillets or chunks, skin-side down, on top of daikon, then pour soy and ginger mixture over them. Add fish stock to pot and bring liquid to a boil. Reduce heat, cover pot, and gently braise fish in liquid for about 20 minutes.

Lift fish and daikon out of pot and transfer to individual plates. Spoon a little cooking liquid over each portion and garnish with cilantro. Spoon remaining cooking liquid over an accompanying bowl of steamed rice, or serve it as a broth.

Serves 4

japanese swordfish kebabs with teriyaki sauce

see variations page 157

In Japan, these kebabs are served as a snack to be enjoyed with the local beer or sake.

2 lbs. swordfish, cut into bite-size cubes
12 bamboo skewers, soaked in water
1 cup Japanese teriyaki sauce (page 60)
small bunch fresh cilantro, coarsely chopped

small bunch fresh flat leaf parsley, coarsely
    chopped
1 lime, cut into wedges

Thread swordfish pieces onto bamboo skewers. Divide the teriyaki sauce into two portions—3/4 cup for brushing on the fish before and during cooking and 1/4 cup to serve. Brush the swordfish pieces with a generous portion of the teriyaki sauce. Place over a prepared charcoal grill or under a conventional broiler, and cook for 2 minutes per side, continually brushing fish with the remaining larger portion of teriyaki sauce.

Transfer immediately to a serving dish and garnish with cilantro and parsley. Serve with lime wedges to squeeze over them and the reserved 1/4 cup sauce for dipping.

Serves 4

variations

indonesian fish & star fruit stew

see base recipe page 129

indonesian fish stew with mango
Replace star fruit with 2 firm, ripe mangos, peeled, pitted, and thickly sliced.

indonesian fish stew with pineapple
Replace star fruit with bite-size chunks of 1 small fresh pineapple.

filipino fish & star fruit stew
Replace galangal, turmeric, and candlenuts in spice paste with a small bunch of finely chopped fresh cilantro and 2 teaspoons sugar.

thai fish & coconut stew with lime leaves
Stir spice paste in oil until fragrant, then pour in 1 (14-ounce) can unsweetened coconut milk mixed with equal amount of water. Add 1/2 fresh coconut, finely sliced or grated, and 4–6 lime leaves with gingerroot and lemongrass. Omit star fruit.

cambodian fish stew with coconut milk
Double quantity of galangal in spice paste, and add 2 lemongrass stalks, finely chopped, and a small bunch fresh cilantro, finely chopped. Add 2 teaspoons palm sugar (or other sugar) when stir-frying spice paste and cook until fragrant. Pour in 1 (14-ounce) can unsweetened coconut milk mixed with equal amount of water. Omit lemongrass and gingerroot.

vietnamese fish steamed with beer

see base recipe page 130

crab steamed with beer
Clean 2–4 fresh crabs and rub with salt and pepper. Put in steamer basket. Scatter with half the scallions, gingerroot, chiles, and herbs, and stir rest into beer. Steam 10–15 minutes, depending on crab size.

lobster steamed with beer
Follow variation above, using fresh lobsters.

mussels steamed with beer
Replace fish with roughly 30 cleaned fresh mussels with tightly closed shells. Place in steamer basket; scatter with half the scallions, gingerroot, chiles, and herbs; and stir the rest into beer. Steam 5–10 minutes, until all shells have opened (discard any that have not).

fish steamed with rice wine
Follow basic recipe, but replace beer with rice wine (dilute with water if you prefer), or dry white wine.

shrimp steamed with rice wine
Replace fish with roughly 25–30 shrimp, cleaned but not shelled. Replace beer with rice wine or dry white wine. Place shrimp in steamer basket. Scatter with half the scallions, gingerroot, chiles, and herbs, and stir the rest into wine. Steam 5–10 minutes.

variations

cambodian fish baked in coconut custard

see base recipe page 133

fish baked in red coconut custard

Replace Cambodian herbal paste with 1–2 tablespoons red Thai curry paste. Tuck a few lime leaves around fish before cooking.

fish baked in green coconut custard

Replace herbal paste with 1–2 tablespoons green Thai curry paste. Tuck a few lime leaves around fish before cooking.

shrimp in green coconut custard

Replace fish with roughly 1 1/2 pounds fresh shrimp, cleaned and shelled. Replace herbal paste with 1–2 tablespoons green Thai curry paste. Add 3–4 crushed lime leaves to dish before cooking.

shrimp & bamboo shoots in red curry custard

Replace fish with 1 pound cleaned and shelled fresh shrimp and 1/2 pound bamboo shoots. Replace herbal paste with 1–2 tablespoons red Thai curry paste.

chili fish baked in coconut custard with lime

Add 1–2 teaspoons chili powder to basic custard for a fiery dish. Serve with wedges of fresh lime.

saigon shrimp curry

see base recipe page 134

red thai shrimp curry

Omit chiles and replace curry powder with 1–2 tablespoons red Thai curry paste. Replace juice and zest of 1 lime with a handful of lime leaves.

cambodian shrimp curry

Replace gingerroot with 1 1/2 ounces galangal, peeled and roughly chopped, and double the quantity of lemongrass. Omit curry powder.

indonesian shrimp curry with chiles

Omit curry powder and double the quantity of chiles. Serve with fresh green chiles, seeded and sliced lengthwise.

shrimp curry with pineapple

Add 4 slices of fresh pineapple, cored and cut into small bite-size pieces, to the ingredients. Toss pineapple in spicy mixture in pan just before pouring in the coconut milk.

shrimp curry with mango

Add flesh of 1 medium-sized fresh, ripe mango, cut into bite-size chunks, to spice paste before stirring in the coconut milk.

variations

malaysian grilled tamarind shrimp

see base recipe page 137

grilled shrimp with lemongrass & gingerroot
Add 1 ounce fresh gingerroot, peeled and grated, and 2 lemongrass stalks, trimmed and finely chopped, to marinade. Proceed with basic recipe.

chili shrimp with tamarind & cilantro
Add 1–2 teaspoons chili oil to marinade along with 2 teaspoons palm sugar and a small bunch of fresh cilantro, finely chopped. Omit fresh cilantro and fresh chiles for serving.

grilled shrimp with garlic & lime
Add 2 cloves garlic, crushed, to marinade and replace tamarind paste with juice of 2 limes.

grilled shrimp with black bean paste
Replace tamarind paste with 1–2 tablespoons commercial black bean paste.

grilled scallops with garlic & lime
Replace shrimp with same quantity of fresh large scallops. Add 2 cloves garlic, crushed, to basic marinade and replace tamarind paste with juice of 2 limes.

singapore chile crab

see base recipe page 138

chile shrimp with parsley & mint
Replace crab with 24 shrimp, cleaned but still in shells. Omit deep-frying.
Toss shrimp in sauce in wok before adding stock. Omit eggs, scallions, and
cilantro. Garnish with finely chopped flat-leaf parsley and mint leaves.

chile scallops with rice wine
Replace crabs with 12–16 scallops. Omit deep-frying; just toss scallops in
sauce. Pour in 1/2 cup chicken stock and 1/2 cup rice wine or dry white
wine. Omit eggs and scallions.

chile mussels with rice wine
Replace crabs with 20–30 mussels, well cleaned with tightly closed shells.
Omit deep-frying. Toss mussels in spicy mixture. Pour in 1/2 cup chicken
stock and 1/2 cup rice wine, or replace both with dry white wine. Omit eggs
and scallions.

baked chile fish
Heat spice paste in wok with other ingredients, then let it cool. Place 8 fish
fillets in ovenproof dish, sprinkle with sea salt, and spread sauce over them.
Pour half the stock into dish, cover dish with foil, and cook at 350ºF for
30–35 minutes. Serve garnished with fresh cilantro. Omit scallions and eggs.

filipino squid stuffed with ham & breadcrumbs

see base recipe page 141

gingerroot squid stuffed with ham & breadcrumbs
Add 1 ounce fresh gingerroot, peeled and finely chopped, and 1 teaspoon cumin seeds to shallots and garlic. Replace bay leaves in stock with an extra piece of gingerroot, peeled and sliced. Garnish with finely chopped fresh cilantro.

squid stuffed with shiitake mushrooms
Follow basic recipe but replace ham with 6 ounces shiitake mushrooms, soaked in water for 20 minutes, drained, trimmed, and finely chopped.

vietnamese squid stuffed with shiitake mushrooms & noodles
Replace ham with 4 ounces shiitake mushrooms, soaked, drained, trimmed, and finely chopped. Replace breadcrumbs with 4 ounces cooked egg or rice noodles, chopped.

squid stuffed with herbs & breadcrumbs
Omit ham. Replace small bunch parsley with a big bunch of flat-leaf parsley, cilantro, mint, and basil leaves, finely chopped, to stuffing.

variations

chinese salt & pepper squid

see base recipe page 142

salt & pepper shrimp
Replace squid with 1 pound shelled and deveined shrimp, with tails. Proceed with basic recipe.

salt & pepper fish
Replace squid with 4–6 fish fillets, cut into thick strips or bite-size chunks. Remove any bones and proceed with basic recipe.

salt & pepper scallops
Replace squid with 1 pound fresh scallops. Proceed with basic recipe.

chili, coriander & cumin squid
Reduce amount of salt to 2 teaspoons and reduce pepper to a grinding. Add 2 teaspoons ground cumin, 1 teaspoon ground coriander, and 1 teaspoon chili powder to flour and proceed with basic recipe.

chili, coriander & cumin shrimp
Follow the variation above for seasoned flour mixture. Replace squid with 1 pound fresh shrimp, shelled to their tails. Proceed with basic recipe and garnish with fresh cilantro, finely chopped.

korean spicy fish braised with daikon

see base recipe page 144

spicy fish braised with white wine & parsley
Follow basic recipe. Reduce the stock to 1 1/4 cups and add the same amount of dry white wine. Garnish with finely chopped flat-leaf parsley instead of cilantro.

japanese spicy fish braised with sake & scallions
Follow basic recipe, but replace stock with sake. Replace cilantro with garnish of 2–3 scallions, trimmed and finely sliced.

korean spicy fish braised with turnip
Replace daikon with fresh turnip, peeled, quartered, and thickly sliced. Proceed with basic recipe.

korean spicy fish braised with pumpkin
Replace daikon with fresh pumpkin, peeled, seeds and membrane removed, and thickly sliced. Proceed with basic recipe.

korean spicy fish braised with sweet potato
Replace daikon with sweet potato, peeled and sliced. Proceed with basic recipe.

korean spicy fish braised with winter melon
Replace daikon with winter melon, peeled, seeds removed, and thickly sliced. Proceed with basic recipe.

variations

japanese swordfish kebabs with teriyaki sauce

see base recipe page 147

japanese shrimp kebabs with teriyaki sauce
Replace swordfish with roughly 1 1/2 pounds fresh, shelled shrimp. Proceed with basic recipe.

japanese scallop kebabs with teriyaki sauce
Replace swordfish with 2 pounds of fresh scallops. Proceed with basic recipe.

japanese scallop kebabs with wasabi dipping sauce
Replace swordfish with fresh scallops. Replace teriyaki sauce with a dipping sauce made from scant 1 cup soy sauce combined with 1 ounce fresh wasabi, finely grated. Brush scallops with dipping sauce instead of teriyaki sauce and serve with reserved sauce.

shrimp & scallop kebab with teriyaki & gingerroot sauce
Replace swordfish with 1/2 pound fresh, shelled shrimp and 1 pound large fresh scallops. Add 1 1/2 ounces fresh gingerroot, peeled and grated, to teriyaki sauce and proceed with basic recipe.

swordfish kebabs with teriyaki & garlic sauce
Add 2 cloves of fresh garlic, crushed, to teriyaki sauce. Proceed with basic recipe.

beef, lamb & pork

Stir-fried, steamed, or roasted, spicy or sticky sweet, the meat dishes of Asia are varied and tasty. Traditionally, meat was a measure of one's wealth as it was scarce and expensive, but nowadays there are numerous meat dishes.

cantonese roast pork with honey

see variations page 178

This is one of the most common ways of preparing pork at Chinese street stalls and in restaurants. Marinated in honey, rice wine, and soy sauce, the pork can be grilled, fried, or roasted.

3 tbsp. honey (plus 2 tbsp. for brushing)
1 tbsp. hoisin sauce
2 tsp. preserved white bean curd
scant 1/2 cup soy sauce
1 tbsp. rice wine

2 tbsp. granulated or palm sugar
1–2 cloves garlic, crushed
2–3 drops red food coloring (optional)
1 1/4 lbs. pork fillet or rump, cut into long, thick strips

In a bowl, whisk together honey, hoisin sauce, white bean curd, soy sauce, and rice wine. Beat in sugar until it has dissolved, then add garlic. Add food coloring, if desired. Toss pork in marinade, cover, and let marinate in refrigerator for about 6 hours.

Preheat oven to 400°F. Place pork strips on a rack over a roasting pan filled with just enough water to cover the base. Roast pork in oven for about 50 minutes, turning it over and basting with leftover marinade from time to time. When meat is cooked, brush with reserved honey and let sit for 10 minutes. Slice strips finely against grain and serve with steamed rice or bread.

Serves 4

malaysian slow-cooked beef with coconut

see variations page 179

This popular Malay dish is traditionally prepared with water buffalo, which is cooked slowly to achieve the desired tenderness as well as a thick sauce. Modern recipes often use beef instead.

for the spice paste
8–10 dried red chiles, soaked in warm water until soft, deseeded, and squeezed dry
8 shallots, peeled and chopped
4–6 cloves garlic, peeled and chopped
2 oz. fresh galangal, peeled and chopped
1 oz. fresh turmeric, peeled and chopped
1 tbsp. coriander seeds
2 tsp. cumin seeds
1 tsp. black peppercorns

2 1/4 lbs. boneless beef (such as bottom round), cut into bite-size cubes
1/4 lb. fresh coconut, grated
3 tbsp. vegetable or peanut oil
2 onions, peeled, halved lengthwise, and sliced with the grain
3 lemongrass stalks, trimmed, halved, and bruised
2 cinnamon sticks
1 tbsp. tamarind paste
4 cups unsweetened coconut milk
1 tbsp. palm sugar
salt and freshly ground black pepper

Using a mortar and pestle or a blender, pound soaked chiles, shallots, garlic, galangal, and turmeric to a smooth paste. In a small heavy pan, dry-roast coriander and cumin seeds with peppercorns until they give off a nutty aroma. Grind roasted spices to a powder and stir into chile paste. Coat beef cubes in spice paste and put aside to marinate for 1–2 hours. Meanwhile dry-roast grated coconut in a small, heavy pan, until it is golden brown and emits

a nutty aroma. Using a mortar and pestle or a blender, grind roasted coconut until it resembles brown sugar, and put it aside.

Heat oil in a wok or a heavy pan. Add onion, lemongrass, and cinnamon sticks, and fry until onions begin to color. Add beef with all the spice paste and toss it around wok, until lightly browned. Stir in tamarind paste and pour in coconut milk. Bring liquid to a boil, stirring all the time. Reduce heat and simmer gently, until sauce begins thicken. Stir in sugar and ground roasted coconut, and continue to simmer very gently, stirring from time to time, until meat is tender and reduced sauce is very thick. This may take 2–3 hours, depending on cut of meat. Season with salt and black pepper to taste, and serve with fresh crusty bread to mop up sauce.

Serves 6

filipino braised oxtail in peanut sauce

see variations page 180

Filipino cooking incorporates oxtail in numerous ways. The finely ground peanuts enrich the sauce and give this dish its own character. You can grind your own nuts, or purchase powdered peanuts in an Asian market. Banana hearts are found in cans in Asian markets.

1 1/4 lbs. oxtail, cut into 1-inch pieces
1 onion, peeled, halved lengthwise, and sliced
4–5 cloves garlic, peeled and crushed
1 (14-oz.) can plum tomatoes, with juice
2 tbsp. fish sauce
2–3 bay leaves
5 1/2 cups beef stock

1 heaping tbsp. rice flour, toasted until lightly brown
1/4 lb. roasted unsalted peanuts, finely ground
2 banana hearts, sliced finely crosswise into bite-size pieces
sea salt and freshly ground black pepper
filipino lime sauce (page 53)

Heat heavy pan and brown oxtail pieces in their own fat (you may need a little oil, but generally the oxtail renders sufficient fat). Transfer meat to a plate. Heat fat from oxtail (add a little corn or peanut oil if there is not enough) and stir in onion and garlic, until they begin to brown. Add tomatoes, fish sauce, and bay leaves and pour in stock. Return oxtail to pot and bring liquid to a boil. Reduce heat, cover pan, and cook oxtail gently for 3–4 hours, until tender (add a little water if it looks dry). Skim fat off top and, using a slotted spoon, lift oxtail onto a plate. Stir rice flour and ground peanuts into liquid in pot and whisk until fairly smooth. Add sliced banana hearts and simmer for 5–6 minutes, until tender. Season with salt and pepper and slip oxtail back into pot. Simmer for 5 more minutes and serve hot with rice, accompanied by a bowl of Filipino lime sauce to spoon over stew.

Serves 4

vietnamese beef stew with star anise

see variations page 181

Prepared for breakfast, lunch, or supper in the north of Vietnam, this aromatic beef stew is generally served with plain noodles, sticky rice, or with chunks of bread to dip in it.

1 1/4 lbs. lean beef, cut into bite-size cubes
2–3 tsp. ground turmeric
2 tbsp. sesame or vegetable oil
3 shallots, chopped
3 cloves garlic, chopped
2 fresh red chiles, stalks and seeds removed, and chopped
2 stalks lemongrass, cut into several pieces and bruised
1 tbsp. curry powder

4 star anise, roasted and ground to a powder (reserve 1–2 tsp for the end)
2 1/2 cups hot beef or chicken stock, or boiling water
3 tbsp. fish sauce
2 tbsp. soy sauce
1 tbsp. cane or palm sugar
salt and freshly ground pepper, to taste
big bunch of basil leaves, torn off stalk
1 onion, halved and finely sliced
small bunch cilantro leaves, roughly chopped

Toss beef in ground turmeric and put aside. Heat a wok or heavy pan, and pour in oil. Add shallots, garlic, chile, and lemongrass, stirring until they become fragrant. Stir in curry powder and roasted star anise powder, followed by beef. Brown beef a little, then pour in hot stock or water, fish sauce, soy sauce, and sugar. Stir well and bring liquid to a boil. Reduce heat and cook gently for about 40 minutes, until meat is tender and liquid has reduced. Season to taste with salt and pepper, stir in reserved roasted star anise powder, and toss in basil. Transfer stew to serving dish and garnish with sliced onion and cilantro leaves.

Serves 4–6

korean braised beef with gingko nuts

see variations page 182

Traditionally this dish is prepared with short ribs, but you can use a cut of meat of your own choice. Gingko nuts are available in Asian stores and some supermarkets.

for the marinade
generous 1/2 cup soy sauce
generous 1/2 cup sake
2 tbsp. palm sugar
2 tbsp. honey
1 tbsp. sesame oil
4 cloves garlic, crushed
4 scallions, trimmed and finely chopped
freshly ground black pepper

2 1/4 lbs. beef ribs, cut into 2 or 3 pieces, and
   scored with a sharp knife
about 12 gingko nuts, shelled
about 12 shiitake mushrooms, trimmed and
   quartered
1–2 tbsp. roasted sesame seeds

In a bowl, mix together soy sauce, sake, and sugar until sugar has dissolved. Beat in honey and sesame oil, then stir in garlic and scallions. Add generous grinding of black pepper. Place ribs in shallow dish and pour marinade over them, rubbing it into incisions. Let marinate for at least 2–3 hours. Transfer ribs and marinade to a wok or heavy-bottomed pot and pour in roughly 3 1/2 cups of water. Bring liquid to a boil, then reduce heat, partially cover pot, and simmer ribs for 2–3 hours, topping off with more water if necessary. Add gingko nuts and cook for 30 more minutes, then add mushrooms and cook for 15 minutes. Transfer ribs to a serving plate and sprinkle with toasted sesame seeds.

Serves 4

japanese beef & scallion rolls

see variations page 183

These beef rolls filled with scallions are typical of Japanese fare—delicate to the eye and subtle to taste. To slice the beef finely, partially freeze it first to keep it firm, or look for ready-prepared slices in the Asian markets.

16 fresh scallions, trimmed at both ends but
    kept long
scant 1 cup mirin
1/2 cup sake
scant 1/2 cup soy sauce

1 lb. marbled beef, cut into wide, paper-thin
    strips
peanut or vegetable oil
1 tbsp. roasted sesame seeds

Blanch scallions in boiling water for 1 minute, then drain and refresh under running cold water. In a bowl, combine mirin, sake, and soy sauce. Add drained scallions. Cover and put aside to marinate for 2–3 hours.

Place 3–4 strips of beef on flat surface, overlapping each other slightly, so that bed of beef is length of scallions. Drain scallions from marinade, reserving marinade. Lay 3 scallions along center of beef bed. Roll beef over scallions to form a long, tight log, and tie with string to prevent it from unrolling. Repeat with remaining beef slices and scallions. Place beef rolls in a dish and pour marinade over them. Cover and refrigerate for 2–3 hours.

Lightly oil a skillet or nonstick broiling pan. Lift beef rolls from marinade and sear over a high heat until crisp. Transfer crisp rolls to a board and cut into 4–5 equal pieces. Place upright in a serving dish so you can see scallion filling, and sprinkle lightly with roasted sesame seeds.

Serves 4

singapore five-spice lamb rolls

see variations page 184

A great favorite at the Malay and Chinese hawker stalls in Singapore, these deep-fried steamed rolls are delicious served with a relish or with a dipping sauce. Fresh bean curd sheets are available in Chinese and Asian markets.

3/4 lb. ground lamb
1 (4-oz.) can water chestnuts, finely chopped
2 tbsp. soy sauce
1 tbsp. sour plum sauce
1/2 tbsp. sesame oil
2 tsp. five-spice powder

1 tsp. glutinous rice flour or cornstarch
1 egg, lightly beaten
4 fresh bean curd sheets, roughly
    7–8 inches square
vegetable oil
1–2 tbsp. Malaysian chile relish (page 49)

Mix ground lamb and water chestnuts in a bowl with soy sauce, sour plum sauce, and sesame oil. Stir in five-spice powder, flour, and egg. With fingers, knead mixture well. Lay bean curd sheets on a flat surface and place equal spoonfuls of lamb mixture on each one, toward edge nearest you. Pull edge over filling, tuck in sides, and roll into a log, like a spring roll. Moisten last edge with a little water to seal roll. Fill a wok a third of the way up with water and place a bamboo steamer over it. Bring water to a boil, then place bean curd rolls in steamer. Cover, reduce heat, and steam for 10–15 minutes to make sure meat is cooked. Remove steamed rolls with tongs and place on a clean dish towel to dry. If you wish, you can let them cool and refrigerate, covered, until ready to fry. Heat enough vegetable oil for deep-frying in a wok. Fry steamed rolls in batches, until crisp and golden. Drain on paper towel and serve whole, or sliced into portions, with a dash of Malaysian chile relish or any dipping sauce of your choice.

Serves 4

indonesian lamb curry

see variations page 185

Slow-cooked with lots of pungent spices, this tender lamb curry is customarily served with sticky or coconut rice and a pickled relish, chile relish, or fresh chiles.

2–3 shallots, peeled and chopped
2–3 cloves garlic, peeled and chopped
3–4 chiles, seeded and chopped
1 oz. fresh galangal, peeled and chopped
1 oz. fresh turmeric, peeled and chopped
1 lemongrass stalk, trimmed and chopped
2–3 candlenuts (or macadamia nuts), finely ground
1–2 tbsp. palm or coconut oil

1 tsp. coriander seeds
1 tsp. cumin seeds
2 tsp. shrimp paste
1 tbsp. palm sugar
1 1/2 lbs. boneless shoulder or leg of lamb, cut into bite-size pieces
1 (14-oz.) can coconut milk
scant 1 cup water
bunch fresh cilantro leaves, roughly chopped

Using a mortar and pestle, pound shallots, garlic, chiles, galangal, turmeric, and lemongrass to a paste. Beat in ground candlenuts. Heat oil in heavy pan, add coriander and cumin seeds, and stir until fragrant. Add shrimp paste and palm sugar and stir-fry for 1–2 minutes, until paste has deepened in color. Add spice paste and stir-fry for another 1–2 minutes, then toss in lamb, making sure pieces are well coated.

Pour in coconut milk and water and bring liquid to a boil. Reduce heat and simmer, covered, gently for 2–3 hours, until meat is very tender (check meat from time to time and add water if it gets a little dry). Toss some chopped cilantro into curry, season with salt and pepper, and tip into a serving dish. Sprinkle remaining cilantro over top and serve with rice and sliced chiles on the side.

Serves 4

cambodian pork &
butternut curry

see variations page 186

Flavored with Cambodian herbal paste, this delicious curry is generally served with rice or chunks of fresh crusty bread to mop up the tasty sauce.

2 tbsp. palm or peanut oil
1 oz. fresh galangal, peeled and finely sliced
2 fresh red chiles, peeled, seeded, and
   finely sliced
3 shallots, peeled, halved, and finely sliced
2 tbsp. Cambodian herbal paste (page 54)
2 tsp. ground turmeric
1 tsp. ground fenugreek
2–3 tsp. palm sugar
1 lb. boneless pork loin, cut into
   bite-size chunks

2 tbsp. fish sauce
3 cups unsweetened coconut milk
1 butternut squash, peeled, seeded, and cut
   into bite-size chunks
4 lime leaves
sea salt
freshly ground black pepper
small bunch fresh cilantro, coarsely chopped
small bunch fresh mint leaves, coarsely chopped

Heat oil in wok or heavy pan. Add galangal, chiles, and shallots, and stir until fragrant. Add herbal paste and stir until it begins to color. Add turmeric, fenugreek, and sugar. Stir in pork, tossing it in spices until golden brown. Stir in fish sauce, pour in coconut milk, and bring liquid to a boil. Add squash and lime leaves and reduce heat.

Cook gently, uncovered, for 15–20 minutes, until squash and pork are tender. Season to taste with salt and pepper. Garnish with cilantro and mint, and serve with noodles, rice, or bread.

Serves 4–6

thai red pork curry

see variations page 187

Colored and flavored with the ubiquitous red curry paste, this curry is enhanced with the additional flavorings of coriander, cumin, turmeric, and mace, displaying the Indian influence in the northern region of Thailand.

2 tsp. coriander seeds
1 tsp. cumin seeds
1–2 pieces of mace
2 tsp. ground turmeric
1–2 tbsp. ghee or peanut oil
2 cloves garlic, finely chopped
2 shallots, finely chopped
1 tbsp. red curry paste
1 tbsp. shrimp paste
1 tbsp. palm sugar or honey

2 lbs. pork fillet or shoulder, cut into
    bite-size pieces
3 cups pork or chicken stock
4 kaffir lime leaves, lightly crushed in
    your hand
1/2 lb. fresh snake beans, trimmed,
    or green beans
sea salt
freshly ground black pepper
small bunch purple basil leaves, shredded

Grind coriander and cumin seeds with mace, then mix with turmeric.

Heat oil in wok or heavy-based pot, add garlic and shallots, and stir until golden. Add ground spices, stirring until fragrant, then stir in red curry paste, shrimp paste, and sugar. Toss in pork, making sure it is well coated, then add stock and lime leaves. Bring liquid to a boil, then reduce heat and cook gently for about 1 hour.

Add snake beans and cook for 30 more minutes, until tender. Season with salt and pepper, stir in half the basil, and garnish with the rest. Serve hot with jasmine rice.

Serves 4

variations

cantonese roast pork with honey

see base recipe page 159

barbecued pork with honey
After marinating pork, prepare a charcoal grill. String strips of pork on skewers. Cook pork over charcoal for about 10 minutes. Brush on remaining marinade as they cook and turn over while cooking. Brush with honey and serve.

roast pork ribs with honey
Follow basic recipe, but replace pork fillet with 1 1/2 pounds pork ribs. After marinating ribs, place in an ovenproof dish, drizzle with a little peanut or vegetable oil, and roast in 400°F oven.

chili roast pork with honey
Replace hoisin sauce with 2 teaspoons chili sauce. Proceed with basic recipe.

roast beef with honey & ginger
Replace pork with same quantity of lean beef, cut into strips. Add 1 1/2 ounces fresh gingerroot, peeled and grated, to marinade. Omit food coloring. Proceed with basic recipe.

roast beef with garlic & lemongrass
Replace pork with same quantity of lean beef, cut into strips. Add 2 lemongrass stalks, trimmed and finely chopped, to marinade. Omit food coloring. Proceed with basic recipe.

malaysian slow-cooked beef with coconut

see base recipe page 160

malaysian slow-cooked lamb with coconut
Replace beef with same quantity of lamb, preferably from shoulder or leg. Proceed with basic recipe.

slow-cooked pork with coconut
Replace beef with same quantity of pork, from rump or leg. Proceed with basic recipe.

slow-cooked pork with pineapple
Replace beef with same quantity of pork. Proceed with basic recipe, omitting coconut. Add half a fresh pineapple, cored and pounded to a pulp, for the last 20 minutes of cooking time.

slow-cooked beef with green mango
Prepare basic recipe, omitting coconut. Add 1 green mango, peeled, pitted, and shredded, to pot for the last 20 minutes of cooking time.

filipino slow-cooked pork with coconut vinegar
Replace beef with same quantity of pork. Replace tamarind paste with 2 tablespoons coconut vinegar. Serve dish with wedges of lime to squeeze over it.

filipino braised oxtail in peanut sauce

see base recipe page 163

oxtail braised with snake beans
Replace banana hearts with 1/2 pound snake beans, cut into bite-size pieces, added in last 10 minutes of cooking.

oxtail braised with eggplant
Replace banana hearts with 8 Asian eggplants, halved or whole, added in last 15 minutes of cooking.

lamb shanks braised with eggplant
Replace oxtail with 4–6 lamb shanks. Replace banana hearts with 8 Asian eggplants, left whole, added 15 minutes before serving.

pork fillet braised with banana blossom hearts
Replace oxtail with 1 pound boneless loin of pork, kept whole. Reduce cooking time to 1–2 hours. Slice pork before serving.

pork loin braised with snake beans & eggplant
Replace oxtail with 1 pound boneless loin of pork, kept whole. Reduce cooking time to 1–2 hours. Omit banana hearts. Add 6–8 snake beans, trimmed to bite-size pieces, and 4 Asian eggplants, halved, for last 15 minutes of cooking.

vietnamese beef stew with star anise

see base recipe page 164

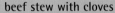

beef stew with cloves
Replace star anise with 1–2 teaspoons whole cloves, roasted. Add them to wok with curry powder.

beef stew with gingerroot
Replace star anise with 2 ounces fresh gingerroot, peeled and grated, added to wok with shallots and garlic. Stir in 1/2 teaspoon ground ginger toward the end of cooking time.

lamb stew with cinnamon
Replace beef with same quantity of lean shoulder of lamb, cut into bite-size pieces. Omit star anise and add 2–3 cinnamon sticks to wok with curry powder.

pork stew with honey & gingerroot
Replace beef with same quantity of boneless loin of pork, cut into bite-size chunks. Omit star anise and add 2 ounces fresh gingerroot, peeled and grated, to wok with shallots and garlic. Replace sugar with 1–2 tablespoons honey.

pork stew with star anise
Replace beef with same quantity of boneless loin of pork, cut into bite-size chunks.

variations

korean braised beef with gingko nuts

see base recipe page 167

korean braised beef with water chestnuts
Replace gingko nuts and shiitake mushrooms with 1 (8-ounce) can water chestnuts, halved. Proceed with basic recipe, adding water chestnuts for the last 25–30 minutes of cooking.

braised pork with water chestnuts
Replace beef ribs with same quantity of pork ribs, left whole. Replace gingko nuts and shiitake mushrooms with 1 (8-ounce) can water chestnuts, halved. Add water chestnuts for the last 25–30 minutes of cooking.

sweet & sour braised beef
Omit gingko nuts and shiitake mushrooms. In the last 15–20 minutes of cooking, stir in 2 tablespoons rice vinegar and 1 tablespoon honey.

sweet & sour braised beef
Omit gingko nuts and shiitake mushrooms. In the last 15–20 minutes of cooking, stir in 2 tablespoons rice vinegar and 2 tablespoons honey.

sweet & sour braised beef with chili
Omit gingko nuts and shiitake mushrooms. In the last 15–20 minutes of cooking, stir in 2 tablespoons rice vinegar, 2 tablespoons honey, and 2 teaspoons chili oil.

variations

japanese beef & scallion rolls

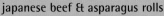

see base recipe page 168

japanese beef & asparagus rolls

Replace scallions with 12 fresh, thin asparagus or 6 thick asparagus, cut in half lengthwise after blanching. Proceed with basic recipe.

beef rolls with nuoc cham

Omit roasted sesame seeds and serve with Vietnamese dipping sauce, nuoc cham (page 57).

beef rolls with coconut vinegar

Omit roasted sesame seeds and serve with Filipino coconut vinegar for dipping.

beef rolls with chile relish

Omit roasted sesame seeds and serve with Malaysian chile relish (page 49).

singapore beef & rice rolls

Omit scallions. Fill beef rolls with 1/2 pound cooked sticky rice, formed into a tightly packed log. Proceed with basic recipe. Serve with soy sauce for dipping.

chinese beef rolls with sweet & sour sauce

Omit scallions. Fill beef rolls with 1/2 pound cooked sticky rice, formed into a tightly packed log. Proceed with basic recipe. Serve with a commercial sweet and sour dipping sauce.

singapore five-spice lamb rolls

see base recipe page 171

five-spice beef rolls
Replace ground lamb with same quantity of lean ground beef.

five-spice pork rolls
Replace ground lamb with same quantity of lean ground pork.

five-spice lamb and peanut rolls
Replace water chestnuts with 1/4 pound shelled, unsalted peanuts.

five-spice lamb & shiitake mushroom rolls
Replace water chestnuts with 1/4 pound dried shiitake mushrooms, soaked
in water for 20 minutes, drained, trimmed, and finely chopped.

lamb rolls with chile & cilantro
Omit five-spice powder and add 1–2 fresh red chiles, seeded and finely
chopped, and a small bunch of fresh cilantro, finely chopped.

pork rolls with peanuts, chile & cilantro
Replace ground lamb with same quantity of lean, ground pork. Replace water
chestnuts with 1/4 pound shelled, unsalted peanuts. Omit five-spice powder
and add 1–2 fresh chiles, seeded and finely chopped, and a small bunch
of fresh cilantro, finely chopped.

variations

indonesian lamb curry

see base recipe page 172

indonesian beef curry
Replace lamb with same quantity of beef rump, or any cut ideal for stewing.

indonesian pork curry
Replace lamb with same quantity of pork. Proceed with basic recipe, reducing cooking time to 1–2 hours.

indonesian goat curry
Replace lamb with same quantity of lean goat meat. Increase quantity of coconut milk to 2 cups.

indonesian lamb curry with gingerroot
Replace galangal and turmeric in the spice paste with 1 1/2 ounces fresh gingerroot, peeled and chopped.

indonesian bison curry
Replace the lamb with the same quantity of bison. Increase the quantity of coconut milk to 1 pint. Proceed with basic recipe.

indonesian lamb curry with peanuts
Replace candlenuts in spice paste with 1/2 cup shelled, unsalted peanuts.

variations

cambodian pork & butternut curry

see base recipe page 175

saigon pork & butternut curry
Follow basic recipe, but replace Cambodian herbal paste with same quantity of a commercial Indian one. Omit cilantro and mint leaves and garnish with 2–3 tablespoons coarsely chopped, roasted unsalted peanuts.

thai pork & butternut curry
Replace Cambodian herbal paste with same quantity of red Thai curry paste. Omit cilantro and mint leaves and garnish with shredded Thai basil leaves.

pork & shrimp curry
Follow basic recipe, but replace butternut squash with 1 pound large shrimp, shelled and deveined. Add shrimp to wok in last 10 minutes of cooking.

pork & sweet potato curry
Replace butternut squash with 2 medium-sized sweet potatoes, peeled and cut into bite-size chunks.

pork & pineapple curry
Replace butternut squash with a small fresh pineapple, skinned, cored, and cut into bite-size chunks. Add pineapple in last 10 minutes of cooking.

thai red pork curry

see base recipe page 176

thai red pork curry with eggplant
Replace snake beans with 4–5 Asian eggplants, halved or quartered lengthwise. Proceed with basic recipe.

thai red pork curry with lemongrass and ginger
Omit dried spices. Add 2 lemongrass stalks, trimmed and finely sliced, to wok with garlic and shallots. Proceed with basic recipe.

thai red pork curry with coconut milk
Prepare basic recipe, replacing pork or chicken stock with same quantity of unsweetened coconut milk.

thai red pork curry with shrimp
Reduce the quantity of pork to 1 1/2 lbs. Replace snake beans with 3/4 pound shelled shrimp. Proceed with basic recipe, adding shrimp to wok for the last 10 minutes of cooking.

thai green pork curry with sweet potato
Replace red Thai curry paste with same quantity of green Thai curry paste. Replace snake beans with 1 medium-sized sweet potato, peeled and cut into bite-size chunks. Proceed with basic recipe.

chicken & duck

Domesticated in parts of Asia for millennia, chickens and ducks feature frequently on the menu. Boiled, steamed, roasted, stir-fried, braised, or broiled, they are celebrated in a myriad of ways, from refined dishes for special occasions to quick, tasty street food.

malaysian devil's hot pot

see variations page 208

Laced with chiles, this hot pot is devilishly hot! A great favorite for family celebrations, it is often served as a meal on its own with breads to mop up the sauce.

10 dried red chiles, soaked in warm water until
    soft, deseeded, and squeezed dry
6 fresh red chiles, seeded and chopped
6–8 shallots, peeled and chopped
6 cloves garlic, peeled and chopped
1 oz. fresh gingerroot, peeled and chopped
6 candlenuts (or macadamia nuts), chopped
2 tsp. ground turmeric
2 tbsp. soy sauce
2 tsp. vinegar
2 tsp. palm sugar
4–6 chicken breasts, or 12 boned chicken
    thighs, cut into bite-size chunks

4 tbsp. palm or peanut oil
1 onion, peeled, halved lengthwise, and sliced
1 oz. fresh gingerroot, peeled and julienned
4 cloves garlic, peeled and cut into strips
2–3 tbsp. rice vinegar
2 tsp. palm sugar
3–4 potatoes, peeled and diced
2 zucchini, partially peeled, halved lengthwise,
    deseeded, and cut into bite-size chunks
6–8 Chinese cabbage leaves, cut into squares
2 tsp. brown mustard seeds, ground to a powder
    and mixed to paste with a little water
salt

Using a mortar and pestle or a blender, pound the chiles, shallots, garlic, gingerroot, and candlenuts to a coarse paste. Stir in turmeric and put aside. Mix soy sauce, vinegar, and palm sugar and rub this marinade into chicken pieces. Let marinate for 30 minutes. Heat oil in a wok or heavy pan. Stir in onion, gingerroot, and garlic and fry until golden. Add spice paste and stir until fragrant. Toss in marinated chicken, until it begins to brown, then pour in enough water to cover. Bring water to a boil, add vinegar and sugar, and stir in potatoes. Reduce heat and cook gently until potatoes are tender. Add zucchini and cook for 2–3 minutes, then stir in cabbage. Stir in mustard paste and season to taste with salt. Serve hot with bread.

Serves 6

indonesian fried chicken

see variations page 209

This unusually crispy chicken is cooked twice—first in spices and flavorings to ensure a depth of taste and then deep-fried to form a crisp, golden skin.

2 shallots, peeled and chopped
4 cloves garlic, peeled and chopped
1 3/4 oz. fresh galangal, peeled and chopped
1 oz. fresh turmeric, peeled and chopped
2 lemongrass stalks, trimmed and chopped

12 chicken thighs or drumsticks, or 6 whole
    chicken legs, separated into drumsticks and
    thighs
2 tbsp. sweet soy sauce
sea salt and freshly ground black pepper
palm or peanut oil

Using a mortar and pestle or a blender, grind shallots, garlic, galangal, turmeric, and lemongrass to a paste.

Place chicken pieces in a heavy pan or earthenware pot, and smear with the spice paste. Add soy sauce and a generous cup of water. Bring liquid to a boil, then reduce heat and cook chicken for about 25 minutes, turning it from time to time, until all the liquid has evaporated. You need the chicken to be dry before deep-frying, but the spices should be sticking to it. Season chicken pieces with salt and pepper.

Heat enough oil for deep-frying in a wok. Fry chicken pieces in batches, until golden brown and crisp. Drain on paper towel and serve hot.

Serves 4

filipino roast chicken with lemongrass & gingerroot

see variations page 210

Spit-roasted in the streets or oven-roasted in the home kitchen for celebratory feasts, variations of aromatic roast chicken can be found all over the Philippines.

3 1/2 oz. fresh gingerroot, peeled and chopped
2–3 lemongrass stalks, trimmed and chopped
3 cloves garlic, peeled and chopped
1/2 cup soy sauce
juice of 1 kalamansi lime (or 1 ordinary lime)
2 tbsp. palm or muscovado sugar
1 organic chicken (about 2 3/4 lbs.)
6 stalks lemongrass, trimmed and bruised

2–3 sweet potatoes, peeled and cut into wedges
1 1/2 oz. gingerroot, peeled and sliced
3–4 tbsp. coconut or peanut oil
sea salt and freshly ground black pepper
1–2 tbsp. palm or granulated sugar
6 tbsp. coconut vinegar or rice vinegar
1–2 fresh red chiles, seeded and finely sliced

Preheat oven to 350°F. Using a mortar and pestle, grind gingerroot, lemongrass, and garlic to a coarse paste. Beat in soy sauce and lime juice. Add sugar, making sure it dissolves. Gently massage skin of chicken to loosen it. Make a few incisions in skin and flesh, then rub gingerroot paste into them and under skin. Place chicken in a roasting pan and stuff with 4 bruised lemongrass stalks. Arrange sweet potatoes around chicken with remaining lemongrass and gingerroot. Drizzle oil over chicken and potatoes and season with salt and pepper. Place pan in oven and roast for just over an hour, until juices run clear. Check chicken after 50 minutes to ensure sugar in paste is not burning, and baste potatoes in roasting juices. The potatoes should caramelize in their own natural sugar. Meanwhile, dissolve sugar in vinegar in a small bowl and stir in chiles. When chicken and potatoes are cooked, serve them immediately with spiked vinegar to splash on top.

Serves 4

thai chicken curry with eggplant

see variations page 211

Like most Thai curries, this recipe is prepared with coconut milk and one of the national curry pastes, which include red, green, and yellow versions. Commercial Thai curry pastes are available in Asian stores and some supermarkets.

1 tbsp. coconut or peanut oil
1–2 tbsp. red Thai curry paste
1–2 tsp. shrimp paste
2–3 lemongrass stalks, trimmed and finely
   sliced
1 red chile, seeded and finely sliced
2 tsp. palm sugar
8 chicken thighs

1 (14-oz.) can unsweetened coconut milk
1 tbsp. fish sauce
8 Asian eggplants, left whole or halved
handful kaffir lime leaves
sea salt
freshly ground black pepper
small bunch fresh cilantro, roughly chopped

Heat oil in a heavy pan, then stir in curry and shrimp pastes. Add lemongrass, chile, and sugar, and stir for 2–3 minutes, until the mixture emits a nutty aroma.

Toss in chicken thighs, coating them in mixture. Pour in coconut milk and fish sauce with scant 1 cup water. Bring liquid to a boil, then add eggplants and lime leaves. Reduce heat and simmer for about 40 minutes.

Season curry with salt and pepper. Garnish with fresh cilantro and serve with steamed jasmine rice.

Serves 4

korean grilled chicken in lettuce leaves

see variations page 212

For this recipe, the chicken can be grilled on the barbecue or broiled in the oven. Like the Vietnamese, the Koreans like to serve grilled dishes with lettuce leaves for wrapping and accompanied by their pickled vegetables, kimchi.

2 whole chicken breasts, cut into 1-inch pieces
2–3 tbsp. soy sauce
1 tbsp. palm or granulated sugar
1 oz. fresh gingerroot, peeled and grated
2 cloves garlic, peeled and crushed

2 scallions, trimmed and finely chopped
1 fresh green chile, seeded and finely chopped
1 tsp. sesame oil
8–12 lettuce leaves, washed and drained

Using the flat side of a cleaver or a butcher's mallet, flatten chicken pieces. In a bowl, whisk together soy sauce and sugar, until sugar has dissolved. Beat in gingerroot, garlic, scallions, chile, and sesame oil. Toss in chicken pieces. Cover and refrigerate for 1–2 hours.

Cook marinated chicken pieces for 3–4 minutes over a charcoal grill or in a lightly oiled broiler pan, turning over to cook both sides. Serve with lettuce leaves for wrapping, kimchi, and Korean dipping sauce (page 58).

Serves 4

cambodian stir-fried chicken

see variations page 213

Gingerroot plays a big role in Cambodian cooking, particularly in stir-fried dishes. Whenever possible, the juicier and more pungent young ginger—available in Asian markets—is used.

2 tbsp. peanut, sesame, or vegetable oil
2–3 cloves garlic, finely sliced in strips
2 oz. fresh young gingerroot, peeled and finely sliced in strips
1–2 fresh Thai chiles, seeded and finely sliced in strips

4 boneless chicken breasts or 4 boned chicken legs, skinned and cut into bite-size chunks
2 tbsp. fish sauce
2 tsp. granulated or palm sugar
freshly ground black pepper
small bunch of cilantro leaves, roughly chopped

Heat a wok or heavy-based pan, then pour in oil. Add garlic, gingerroot, and chile, stirring until fragrant and golden. Add chicken and toss around wok for 1–2 minutes. Stir in fish sauce and sugar, and stir-fry for 4–5 minutes more. Season with pepper and add some of the cilantro. Tip chicken onto a serving dish and garnish with the remaining cilantro. Serve hot with jasmine rice.

Serves 4

japanese chicken with yakitori sauce

see variations page 214

This dish is very popular in Japan and often the chicken livers and gizzards are skewered and served too. You can make your own yakitori sauce or buy a commercially prepared version in Asian markets.

generous 1 cup soy sauce
2 tbsp. tamari sauce
1/2 cup mirin
1/2 cup sake
2 tbsp. rock or palm sugar
2 whole chicken breasts, cut into
  bite-size pieces

4 scallions, trimmed and cut into
  bite-size pieces
generous 1/2 cup chicken livers, cut into
  bite-size pieces

To prepare sauce, put soy sauce, tamari sauce, mirin, sake, and sugar in a heavy pan and bring to a boil. Reduce heat and simmer for about 25–30 minutes until sauce has reduced by half. Let cool in pan.

Thread chicken and scallions, alternately, onto skewers. Thread chicken livers onto separate skewers. Brush chicken and livers with yakitori sauce and cook them under the broiler in a well-oiled broiler pan, or over a charcoal grill, for about 4 minutes, turning over to cook both sides and basting with sauce from time to time. Serve immediately.

Serves 4

cambodian duck stew with snake beans

see variations page 215

Packed with seasonal vegetables and flavor, variations of this stew can be found in neighboring Vietnam, Thailand, and Malaysia. It is delicious served with jasmine rice and a green papaya salad.

2 tbsp. peanut oil or pork fat
4 cloves garlic, halved and smashed
1 oz. fresh galangal, peeled and finely sliced
2 fresh chiles
2–3 tbsp. Cambodian herbal paste (page 54)
1 tbsp. palm sugar
6 duck legs
2 tbsp. fish sauce
2 cups unsweetened coconut milk

3/4 lb. pumpkin flesh, seeds removed, cut into bite-size chunks
1/4 lb. fresh snake beans, trimmed and cut into 2-inch lengths
3 ripe tomatoes, skinned, quartered, and seeded
small bunch basil leaves
sea salt and freshly ground black pepper
small bunch fresh cilantro, coarsely chopped
small bunch mint leaves, coarsely chopped

Heat oil or fat in a wok or heavy pan. Add garlic, galangal, and chiles, and stir until fragrant and golden. Add herbal paste and sugar, stirring until sugar dissolves. Add duck legs, tossing to cover with spices, and stir in fish sauce and coconut milk. Reduce heat and simmer for 10 minutes.

Add pumpkin and snake beans, and cook until tender (if you need more liquid, stir in a little water). Add tomatoes and basil leaves. Cook another 2 minutes, then season to taste with salt and pepper. Garnish with cilantro and mint, and serve hot with jasmine rice.

Serves 4–6

vietnamese roast duck with gingerroot

see variations page 216

This is Vietnam's answer to China's "Peking Duck," which is served in three courses. The Vietnamese, on the other hand, generally serve it as one course with pickled vegetables, dipping sauces, and steamed rice.

for the marinade
2–3 tbsp. fish sauce
2 tbsp. soy sauce
2 tbsp. honey
2 tsp. ground coriander
1 tsp. ground ginger

1 plump duck (about 5 lbs.)
piece of gingerroot, roughly 3 1/2 oz., peeled,
    roughly chopped, and lightly crushed
4 cloves of garlic, peeled and crushed
1 lemongrass stalk, halved and bruised
4 scallions, halved and crushed

In a bowl, beat marinade ingredients together until honey dissolves. Using your fingers, lightly rub duck skin to loosen it, until you can get your fingers between skin and meat. Rub marinade all over duck, inside skin and out. Then place duck on a rack over a tray and refrigerate for 24 hours. If any marinade drips into tray, rub it back over duck. Preheat oven to 425ºF. Stuff gingerroot, garlic, lemongrass, and scallions into cavity and tie legs with string. Using a bamboo or metal skewer, poke holes in skin, including the legs. Place duck, breast-side down, on a rack over a roasting pan and put into oven to roast. Baste it from time to time with juices that drip into pan. After 45 minutes, turn duck breast-side up, baste generously, and return to oven for 45 more minutes, basting every 15 minutes. The duck is ready when juices run clear. Serve immediately, pulling at skin and meat with your fingers, rather than carving it. Serve with jasmine rice and a selection of dipping sauces.

Serves 4–6

singapore stir-fried duck with mango

see variations page 217

Sold at Chinese and Nonya hawker stalls in Singapore, this is a great recipe for using up leftover roast duck. It can be served hot with rice, or at room temperature as a salad.

2–3 tbsp. sesame or peanut oil
1 onion, peeled and thinly sliced
1 red bell pepper, seeded and thinly sliced
generous 1/2 lb. thinly shredded cooked
    duck meat
sea salt

2–3 tbsp. hoisin sauce
1 fresh, firm mango, skinned and cut into thin
    shreds or slices
2 scallions, trimmed and cut into
    bite-size pieces

Heat oil in a wok, add onion and pepper, and stir for 2–3 minutes. Toss in duck meat and season with salt. Stir in hoisin sauce, then toss in mango and scallions for 1 minute. Serve immediately.

Serves 4

variations

malaysian devil's hot pot

see base recipe page 189

devil's hot pot with bok choy
Replace Chinese cabbage leaves with 2–3 bok choy, trimmed and
roughly chopped.

devil's hot pot with sweet potato
Replace potatoes and zucchini with 2 small sweet potatoes, peeled and cut
into bite-size pieces. Proceed with basic recipe, adding sweet potato at the
same time as potatoes.

devil's hot pot with eggplant
Replace zucchini with 6–8 halved small Asian eggplants. Cook for 3–4 minutes
before adding cabbage leaves.

devil's hot pot with duck & pineapple
Replace chicken with 4 duck breasts. Replace zucchini and cabbage with 4–6
slices fresh pineapple, cut into bite-size chunks. Omit mustard seed paste.
Season and garnish with fresh cilantro, coarsely chopped.

devil's hot pot with duck & mango
Replace chicken with 4 duck breasts. Replace zucchini and cabbage with 2 firm,
ripe mangoes, peeled and cut into bite-size chunks. Omit mustard seed paste.
Season and garnish with fresh cilantro, coarsely chopped.

indonesian fried chicken

see base recipe page 190

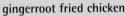

gingerroot fried chicken

Omit turmeric and lemongrass and replace galangal with 2 ounces fresh gingerroot, peeled and chopped. Proceed with basic recipe.

fiery fried chicken

Grind 2–4 fresh red chiles, seeded and roughly chopped, with shallots, garlic, galangal, turmeric, and lemongrass to make a fiery paste. Proceed with basic recipe.

coriander fried chicken

Add 2 teaspoons ground coriander to spice paste. Proceed with basic recipe and garnish chicken with fresh cilantro, coarsely chopped.

tomato & chili fried chicken wings

Add 2 tablespoons tomato paste with 1 tablespoon palm sugar and 1–2 teaspoons chili powder to basic spice paste. Replace chicken thighs with 12 chicken wings and proceed with basic recipe. Drizzle a little chili oil over cooked wings.

cambodian fried frog's legs

Add 2 fresh red chiles, seeded and chopped, to spice paste ingredients. Replace chicken pieces with 12 frog's legs and proceed with basic recipe. Before serving, drizzle legs with a little chili oil.

variations

filipino roast chicken with lemongrass & gingerroot

see base recipe page 193

fiery roast chicken with lemongrass & gingerroot

Add 2 red chiles, seeded and finely chopped, to spice paste. Proceed with basic recipe. Garnish cooked chicken with fresh cilantro, finely chopped.

coriander roast chicken with lemongrass & gingerroot

Reduce gingerroot in paste to 2 ounces, omit lime juice, and add 2 teaspoons ground coriander to spice paste. Proceed with basic recipe.

roast duck with lemongrass & gingerroot

Replace chicken with 2 wild ducks. Reduce cooking time to about 35 minutes, until the skin is nicely browned and the juices run clear.

roast chicken with lemongrass & green mango

Omit gingerroot in the paste and in roasting pan. Combine vinegar with sugar and stir in grated flesh of 1 green mango. Omit chiles. Add a handful of fresh cilantro leaves, finely chopped. Serve as tart relish with roast chicken.

roast chicken with lemongrass & coconut

Omit gingerroot from paste and roasting pan and proceed with basic recipe. Combine vinegar with sugar and stir in grated flesh of half a fresh coconut. Serve with roast chicken.

thai chicken curry with eggplant

see base recipe page 194

thai chicken curry with snake beans
Replace eggplants with 1/2 pound snake beans, trimmed to bite-size pieces.
Proceed with basic recipe and add snake beans to pot for last 15 minutes
of cooking.

thai chicken curry with sweet potato
Replace eggplants with 2 medium-sized sweet potatoes, peeled and cut into
bite-size pieces. Proceed with basic recipe and add sweet potatoes to pot for last
20 minutes.

saigon chicken curry
Replace Thai curry paste with same quantity of commercial Indian curry paste.
Proceed with basic recipe and serve with crusty bread to mop up sauce.

thai chicken curry with pineapple
Proceed with basic recipe. Add half a fresh pineapple, peeled, cored, and cut into
bite-size chunks for last 5–10 minutes of cooking.

thai chicken curry with shrimp
Replace eggplants with 1/2 pound large fresh shrimp, shelled and deveined.
Proceed with basic recipe and add shrimp for last 5–10 minutes of cooking.

variations

korean grilled chicken with lettuce leaves

see base recipe page 197

filipino grilled chicken with lime dipping sauce
Add 2 tablespoons coconut vinegar to marinade. Serve chicken with Filipino lime sauce (page 53).

vietnamese grilled chicken with nuoc cham
Serve chicken with extra green chiles, seeded and sliced; a bunch of flat-leaf parsley leaves for wrapping in lettuce leaves; and Vietnamese dipping sauce (page 57).

malaysian grilled chicken with chile relish
Omit lettuce for wrapping and serve chicken with Malaysian chile relish (page 49).

cambodian grilled chicken
Marinate chicken in Cambodian herbal paste (page 54). Serve chicken with rice or noodles.

grilled chicken with lemongrass & lime
Add 2 lemongrass stalks, finely chopped, to marinade. Serve chicken with wedges of lime.

grilled chicken with rice wrappers
Replace lettuce leaves with rice wrappers (which are commercially available in Asian markets), and serve with a dipping sauce of your choice.

cambodian stir-fried chicken

see base recipe page 198

stir-fried chicken with peanuts
Prepare basic recipe, adding 2–3 tablespoons fresh peanuts, shelled and coarsely chopped, with fish sauce and sugar.

stir-fried chicken with lemongrass
Add 2 lemongrass stalks, finely sliced, to wok with gingerroot and garlic.

stir-fried chicken with soy sauce
Follow basic recipe. Reduce fish sauce to 1 tablespoon and add 2 tablespoons soy sauce at the same time.

stir-fried chicken with scallions
Prepare basic recipe, adding 4 scallions, trimmed and sliced, with fish sauce and sugar.

stir-fried chicken with bean sprouts
Prepare basic recipe, adding 1/2 pound bean sprouts with fish sauce and sugar. Splash in 2 tablespoons soy sauce before serving.

stir-fried chicken with coconut & lime
Prepare basic recipe, adding grated flesh of half a coconut with the fish sauce. Omit sugar and serve with wedges of lime.

variations

japanese skewered chicken with yakitori sauce

see base recipe page 201

japanese skewered chicken with teriyaki sauce

Replace yakitori sauce with Japanese teriyaki sauce (page 60). Proceed with basic recipe.

filipino skewered chicken with lime sauce

Replace yakitori sauce with Filipino lime sauce (page 53). Proceed with basic recipe and serve the chicken with wedges of lime to squeeze over it.

malaysian skewered chicken with chile relish

Replace yakitori sauce with Malaysian chile relish (page 49). Proceed with basic recipe.

indonesian skewered chicken with fiery peanut sauce

Replace yakitori sauce with Indonesian fiery peanut sauce (page 50). Proceed with basic recipe.

cambodian skewered chicken

Replace yakitori sauce with Cambodian herbal paste (page 54). Proceed with basic recipe.

variations

cambodian duck stew with snake beans

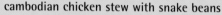
see base recipe page 202

cambodian chicken stew with snake beans
Replace duck with 8 chicken legs. Proceed with basic recipe.

duck stew with turnip & snake beans
Replace pumpkin with same quantity of turnip flesh, peeled and seeded.
Proceed with basic recipe.

duck stew with sweet potatoes
Replace pumpkin with 2–3 medium-sized sweet potatoes, peeled and cut
into bite-size chunks. Omit snake beans and proceed with basic recipe.

duck stew with sweet potatoes & pineapple
Replace pumpkin with 2 small sweet potatoes, peeled and cut into bite-size
pieces. Replace snake beans with 4–6 slices fresh pineapple, cored and cut
into bite-size pieces. Cook sweet potatoes in liquid for about 10 minutes
before adding pineapple. Omit tomatoes and proceed with basic recipe.

chicken stew with sweet potatoes
Replace duck with 8 chicken legs and replace pumpkin with 2 small sweet
potatoes, peeled and cut into bite-size pieces. Proceed with basic recipe.

variations

vietnamese roast duck with gingerroot

see base recipe page 205

malay roast duck with chile relish
Add 2 red chiles, seeded and finely chopped, to marinade. Serve roast duck with Malaysian chile relish (page 49).

korean roast duck with sweet & sour sauce
Prepare a sweet and sour chili sauce by combining 4 tablespoons Korean hot chili bean paste with 2 tablespoons honey and 3 tablespoons rice vinegar. Serve roast duck with this dipping sauce.

roast duck with coconut vinegar
Serve roast duck with coconut vinegar for dipping.

roast duck with teriyaki sauce
Serve roast duck with Japanese teriyaki sauce (page 60). Brush some sauce onto duck and serve the rest for dipping.

roast duck with fiery peanut sauce
Serve roast duck with Indonesian fiery peanut sauce (page 50).

roast duck with lime sauce
Serve roast duck with Filipino lime sauce (page 53).

singapore stir-fried duck with mango

see base recipe page 206

singapore stir-fried duck with soy sauce & honey
Follow basic recipe, replacing hoisin sauce with 2–3 tablespoons soy sauce and 1 tablespoon honey. Omit mango.

chinese stir-fried duck with oyster sauce
Replace hoisin sauce with same quantity of commercial oyster sauce, available in Asian markets. Omit mango and serve with noodles.

vietnamese stir-fried duck with ginger & soy sauce
Add 1 ounce fresh gingerroot, peeled and finely shredded, to wok with onion. Replace hoisin sauce with same quantity of soy sauce.

indonesian stir-fried duck with chili sauce
Follow basic recipe, replacing hoisin sauce with Indonesian sweet soy sauce. Omit mango and serve with commercial chili sauce.

stir-fried duck with chinese sausage
Stir-fry onion and pepper, then toss in 2 Chinese sausages, finely sliced. Add duck and proceed with basic recipe.

stir-fried duck with asian pear
Replace mango with 1 Asian pear, peeled, cored, and finely sliced.

vegetables & salads

Asian eggplants, snake beans, water spinach, bok choy, jicama, mung bean sprouts, winter melon, bamboo shoots, and banana hearts—these are just some of the vegetables found in Asian cooking. Stir-fried, steamed, marinated, and tossed in salad, the variety is astounding.

asian roasted sweet potatoes with peanut sauce

see variations page 238

Served as a side dish or salad, this is a favorite throughout Southeast Asia. Served with sticky rice or chunks of crusty bread, the dish could suffice as a light vegetarian meal.

3 medium-sized sweet potatoes, peeled and cut
    into long strips
2 leeks, trimmed and quartered
2 cloves garlic, peeled and chopped
1 oz. fresh gingerroot, peeled and chopped
sea salt
roughly 4 tbsp. palm, vegetable, or peanut oil
4 cloves garlic, peeled and chopped
2–3 fresh red chiles, seeded and chopped

1 tsp. shrimp paste
1/4 lb. roasted peanuts, crushed
1–2 tbsp. soy sauce
juice of 1 lime
1–2 tsp. rice vinegar
2 tsp. palm sugar or dark honey
sea salt
freshly ground black pepper
2–3 tbsp. roasted peanuts, coarsely ground

Preheat oven to 400°F. Arrange sweet potatoes and leeks in shallow oven dish. Using a mortar and pestle, pound 2 cloves garlic and ginger to a paste, then smear it over vegetables. Sprinkle with a little salt and pour oil on top. Bake for about 45 minutes, until the vegetables are tender and slightly browned. Toss them in oil halfway through cooking. Meanwhile, make sauce. Using a mortar and pestle or a blender, pound 4 cloves garlic and chiles to a paste. Beat in shrimp paste and peanuts. Stir in soy sauce, lime juice, vinegar, and sugar, and blend with a little water until sauce is thick and creamy. Season with salt and pepper and adjust sweet and sour balance to your taste. Arrange roasted vegetables on a plate. Drizzle sauce over them, or serve sauce separately in a bowl. Sprinkle ground peanuts on top and serve warm, or at room temperature, with fresh crusty bread to mop up sauce.

Serves 4–6

chinese stir-fried bok choy with shrimp

see variations page 239

Bok choy, the common Chinese cabbage, is popular in all Chinese cooking. Readily available in Asian markets and supermarkets, it can be served as an accompaniment to a meat or poultry dish, or as a dish on its own.

4 cloves garlic, peeled and chopped
1 oz. fresh gingerroot, peeled and chopped
2 fresh red chiles, stalk and seeds removed, and chopped
2 tbsp. dried shrimp, soaked in warm water to soften, and drained

1 tsp. shrimp paste
2 tbsp. palm, vegetable, or peanut oil
1/2 tbsp. palm sugar
1–2 tbsp. soy sauce
1 lb. bok choy, washed and trimmed
sea salt and freshly ground black pepper

Using a mortar and pestle, pound garlic, gingerroot, and chiles to smooth paste. Add dried shrimp and pound them to paste. Beat in shrimp paste and bind with a little oil.

Heat remaining oil in a wok or heavy pan. Stir in spicy shrimp paste and cook over low heat for 2–3 minutes, until fragrant and beginning to color. Stir in sugar and soy sauce until well mixed. Add bok choy, tossing it around pan to coat leaves in spicy juices until they begin to wilt. Season to taste with salt and pepper and serve immediately.

Serves 2–4

cambodian jungle curry with galangal

see variations page 240

Variations of this fiery, flavorful vegetarian curry spring up all over Cambodia and southern Vietnam. A favorite with the Buddhist monks and countryside stalls, it can be served with rice, noodles, or crusty bread.

2 tbsp. palm or vegetable oil
2 onions, roughly chopped
2 sticks lemongrass, roughly chopped and
    bruised
3–4 fresh green chiles, stalk and seeds removed,
    and finely sliced
thumb-sized knob of galangal, peeled
    and chopped
2–3 carrots, peeled, halved lengthwise
    and sliced
1/4 lb. long green snake beans
grated zest of 1 lime
2 tsp. soy sauce

1 tbsp. rice vinegar
2 tsp. fish sauce
1 tsp. black peppercorns, crushed with mortar
    and pestle
1 tbsp. palm sugar
1–2 tsp. ground turmeric
1 (4-oz.) can bamboo shoots
large handful of fresh spinach leaves, steamed
    and roughly chopped
1/2 cup unsweetened coconut milk
sea salt
small bunch fresh cilantro, roughly chopped
small bunch fresh mint, roughly chopped

Heat wok, then add oil. Once hot, stir in onions, lemongrass, chiles, and galangal. Add carrots and snake beans with lime zest, and cook for 1–2 minutes. Stir in soy sauce, rice vinegar, and fish sauce. Add crushed peppercorns, sugar, and turmeric, then stir in bamboo shoots, followed by spinach. Pour in coconut milk and blend mixture together. Cook for about 10 minutes, season with salt, and serve hot, garnished with fresh cilantro and mint.

Serves 4

singapore fried eggplant with spicy garlic sauce

see variations page 241

Served with coconut rice, or as an accompaniment to grilled meat and poultry, this dish is popular at the hawker stalls in Singapore. Generally, the eggplants are deep-fried, but if you prefer, you can bake them in the oven.

6 shallots, peeled and chopped
4 cloves garlic, peeled and chopped
2 fresh red chiles, stalk and seeds removed, and chopped
1 stalk lemongrass, trimmed and chopped
1 tsp. shrimp paste
1 tbsp. sesame oil
1–2 tbsp. soy sauce

1/2 tbsp. palm or granulated sugar
vegetable oil
2 long, slender, purple eggplants, partially peeled in strips and halved lengthwise
1 fresh green chile, stalk and seeds removed, finely chopped
small bunch fresh mint, finely chopped
small bunch fresh cilantro, finely chopped

Using a mortar and pestle, pound shallots, garlic, chiles, and lemongrass to a paste. Beat in shrimp paste and mix well. Heat sesame oil in a small wok or heavy pan. Stir in spicy paste and cook until fragrant and brown. Stir in soy sauce and sugar and cook until mixture resembles a sauce. Turn off heat. Heat enough oil for deep-frying in a wok or heavy pan. Drop in eggplants and fry on both sides until tender. Drain on paper towel and press down the center of each half to make a dip or shallow pouch to hold the sauce. Arrange eggplant halves on a plate and smear with the spicy sauce. Garnish with chopped green chile, mint, and cilantro and serve at room temperature.

Serves 2–4

vietnamese stir-fried tofu with basil

see variations page 242

There are numerous ways of preparing tofu in Asia, but this is a particularly delicious one. Serve it on its own or with stir-fried noodles or rice, or as part of a vegetarian meal.

3/4 lb. tofu
3 lemongrass stalks, trimmed and finely
    chopped
3 tbsp. soy sauce
1–2 fresh red chiles, stalk and seeds removed,
    and finely chopped

2 cloves garlic, crushed
1 tsp. ground turmeric
2 tsp. palm or granulated sugar
sea salt
2 tbsp. sesame or peanut oil
small bunch of basil leaves

Rinse, drain, and pat dry tofu. Cut into bite-size cubes. In a bowl, mix lemongrass, soy sauce, chile, garlic, and turmeric with sugar until the sugar has dissolved. Add a little salt to taste and toss in tofu, making sure it is well coated. Let marinate for an hour.

Heat a wok or heavy-based pan. Pour in oil, then stir in marinated tofu, turning it frequently to make sure it is cooked evenly. Toss in most of the basil leaves. Tip tofu onto a serving dish, scatter remaining basil over top, and serve hot or at room temperature.

Serves 3–4

red thai eggplant curry

see variations page 243

Eggplant curries are popular throughout Asia, the Thai version being the most famous. Generally enriched with coconut milk and warming spices, the Thai version is bittersweet from the kaffir lime leaves with a hint of licorice from the basil.

1 tbsp. vegetable oil
4 cloves garlic, crushed
2 shallots, peeled and sliced
2 dried chiles, left whole
3 tbsp. red Thai curry paste
1 tbsp. shrimp paste
1 tbsp. palm sugar

2 cups unsweetened coconut milk
1 generous cup chicken stock or water
3 eggplants, cut into bite-size pieces, or
    12 small Asian eggplants, halved
6 fresh kaffir lime leaves
bunch of fresh basil leaves
2 limes, quartered

Heat oil in a wok or heavy pan. Stir in garlic, shallots, and chiles until they begin to color. Stir in curry paste, shrimp paste, and palm sugar until mixture begins to darken. Add coconut milk and stock, then toss in eggplant pieces and lime leaves.

Partially cover pan, and cook eggplants over a gentle heat for about 25 minutes, until tender. Stir in basil leaves and check seasoning. Serve with jasmine rice and lime wedges to squeeze over curry.

Serves 4–6

korean stir-fried potatoes

see variations page 244

This delicious dish of stir-fried potatoes is often served on its own as a snack with pickled vegetables. It is also a tasty accompaniment to a number of curries and grilled dishes.

2 tbsp. sesame or peanut oil
2 cloves garlic, finely chopped
1/2 lb. potatoes, peeled and cut into
    bite-size cubes
1-2 fresh chiles, seeded and finely chopped

2-3 tbsp. soy sauce
2 tsp. honey
small bunch fresh cilantro, finely chopped
1 tbsp. roasted sesame seeds

Heat oil in a wok or heavy pan and add garlic, stirring until it just begins to turn golden. Toss in potatoes with chiles and stir-fry for 5-6 minutes. Add soy sauce and continue to stir-fry until liquid is absorbed and potatoes begin to crispen. Add honey and stir-fry for a further 1-2 minutes. Toss in cilantro and serve immediately with a sprinkling of sesame seeds on top.

Serves 4

green papaya salad

see variations page 245

The tart, crunchy flesh of green papayas complements spicy grilled or stir-fried dishes beautifully. This Filipino version is sweet and sour, but there are many variations throughout Asia.

2 firm green papayas, seeded, peeled, and grated
4 shallots, peeled and finely sliced
1–2 fresh red chiles, seeded, halved lengthwise, and finely sliced
1 generous cup plump raisins

2 cloves garlic, peeled and crushed
1 oz. fresh gingerroot, peeled and grated
3–4 tbsp. coconut vinegar
1–2 tbsp. palm sugar
small bunch of cilantro leaves, coarsely chopped

Put papayas, shallots, chiles, raisins, garlic, and gingerroot into a bowl. In a separate bowl, beat coconut vinegar with sugar until the sugar has dissolved.

Pour sweetened vinegar over salad and toss well. Let salad sit for at least an hour so flavors mingle, then garnish with cilantro before serving.

Serves 4

indonesian mango, pineapple & bean sprout salad

see variations page 246

This refreshing fruity salad appears in its many guises in Indonesia and Malaysia. Designed to be flexible, it is tossed in a pungent and tangy dressing and can include any choice of fruit and vegetables you like.

1/2 lb. roasted peanuts
4 cloves garlic, peeled and chopped
2–4 fresh red chiles, seeded and chopped
2 tsp. shrimp paste, dry-roasted in pan over
   high heat
1 tbsp. tamarind paste
2 tbsp. palm sugar
sea salt

1 small cucumber, partially peeled, deseeded,
   and finely sliced
1 jicama, peeled and finely sliced
1 green mango, peeled and finely sliced
2 star fruit, finely sliced
1/2 pineapple, finely sliced and cut into
   bite-size pieces
1/2 lb. bean sprouts, rinsed and drained

Using a mortar and pestle or a food processor, pound peanuts with garlic and chiles to a coarse paste. Beat in roasted shrimp paste, tamarind paste, and sugar. Add enough water to make a thick, pouring sauce, and stir until sugar has dissolved. Add salt to taste.

Put fruit and vegetables into a serving bowl. Pour in some of the sauce and toss gently. Let salad stand for 30 minutes, then scatter bean sprouts over top. Serve with remaining sauce drizzled over top.

Serves 4–6

japanese bamboo shoot & shiitake salad

see variations page 247

The crunchy texture of bamboo shoots is prized for salads and stir-fries in Japan. Fresh bamboo shoots, which need to be boiled for 15 minutes before using, are available in some Asian markets, but canned bamboo shoots are available in all supermarkets.

10 fresh shiitake mushrooms, blanched and
    drained
3 bamboo shoots, blanched and drained
1/4 cup mirin
1/4 cup soy sauce

1 tbsp. rice vinegar
2 tsp. sesame oil
freshly ground black pepper
2 scallions, trimmed and finely sliced
small bunch fresh cilantro, finely chopped

Slice shiitake mushrooms finely and put into a serving bowl. Cut bamboo shoots in half lengthwise, then slice thinly and add to bowl.

Mix together mirin, soy sauce, vinegar, and sesame oil. Pour it over mushrooms and bamboo shoots. Add a good grinding of pepper and most of the scallions and toss well. Cover salad and let it marinate for 30 minutes.

In same serving bowl or individual bowls, scatter remaining scallions over salad and garnish with cilantro.

Serves 4

variations

asian roasted sweet potatoes with peanut sauce

see base recipe page 219

roasted sweet potatoes with malaysian chile relish
Prepare basic recipe. Replace peanut sauce with fiery Malaysian chile relish
(page 49).

roasted sweet potatoes with korean dipping sauce
Prepare basic recipe. Replace peanut sauce with tangy Korean dipping sauce
(page 58).

roasted sweet potatoes & apple with peanut sauce
Follow basic recipe, replacing leeks with 2 crisp apples, peeled, cored, and sliced.

roasted sweet potatoes, carrots & onions with peanut sauce
Follow basic recipe, replacing leeks with 2–3 carrots, peeled and cut into thick
sticks, and 2 onions, peeled and quartered.

roasted sweet potatoes & eggplant with peanut sauce
Follow basic recipe, replacing leeks with 1 large eggplant, cut into long
thick sticks.

roasted eggplant & zucchini with peanut sauce
Follow basic recipe, replacing sweet potato and leeks with 2 eggplants, halved
and cut into sticks, and 2 zucchini, halved and cut into sticks.

variations

chinese stir-fried bok choy with shrimp

see base recipe page 220

chinese bok choy with oyster sauce
Follow basic recipe, replacing sugar and soy sauce with 2 tablespoons
commercial oyster sauce.

stir-fried bok choy with dried mushrooms
Soak 1/4 pound dried shiitake mushrooms in a little water for 20 minutes.
Drain, trim, and chop mushrooms and add them to shrimp paste in wok. Add
bok choy, cooking until it wilts, and splash 1–2 tablespoons soy sauce into
wok. Serve immediately.

stir-fried bok choy with lemon
Omit sugar and soy sauce from spicy shrimp paste in wok. Stir-fry bok
choy until it begins to wilt. Toss in juice and finely sliced rind of 1 lemon
and serve immediately.

vegetarian stir-fried bok choy with lemongrass
Omit shrimp paste and shrimp and use 1–2 lemongrass stalks, trimmed and
finely chopped, instead. Proceed with basic recipe.

stir-fried spinach with shrimp
Follow basic recipe for spicy shrimp paste. Toss 1/2 pound fresh shelled shrimp
into the spice paste in wok and proceed with basic recipe, replacing bok choy
with fresh spinach.

variations

cambodian jungle curry with galangal

see base recipe page 223

vegetarian jungle curry
For a vegetarian version, omit fish sauce. Adjust salt to your taste.

jungle curry with kaffir lime leaves
Add 4–6 kaffir lime leaves, crushed in your hand to release the flavor, to wok with carrots and snake beans. Omit lime zest and mint and cilantro garnish.

jungle curry with bean sprouts
Proceed with basic recipe, stirring in generous handful of bean sprouts for last 2 minutes of cooking time. Scatter a few more sprouts with cilantro to garnish dish. Omit mint.

jungle curry with fresh coconut
Add grated flesh of 1/2 coconut with bamboo shoots. Omit spinach and mint.

sweet potato curry with galangal
Replace carrots with 1 sweet potato, peeled and cut into bite-size pieces.

papaya curry with galangal
Omit carrots and spinach. Cut flesh of 2 ripe but firm papayas, peeled and with seeds removed, into bite-size pieces. Add them to wok with bamboo shoots. Omit mint.

singapore fried eggplant with spicy garlic sauce

see base recipe page 224

baked eggplant with spicy garlic sauce
Instead of deep-frying eggplant, place eggplant halves on a lightly oiled baking pan and bake at 350°F for 30–40 minutes, until tender. Press the center of the baked flesh to make a dip and spoon sauce into it. Serve hot, at room temperature, or cold.

fried eggplant with fiery peanut sauce
Replace spicy garlic sauce with Indonesian fiery peanut sauce (page 50). Proceed with basic recipe.

fried sweet potatoes with spicy garlic sauce
Replace eggplants with 2 medium-sized sweet potatoes, peeled and quartered lengthwise, and proceed with basic recipe.

baked sweet potatoes with spicy garlic sauce
Replace eggplants with 2 medium-sized sweet potatoes, peeled and quartered lengthwise. Bake sweet potatoes at 350°F for about 40 minutes, until tender. Follow basic recipe for serving.

fried zucchini with spicy garlic sauce
Replace eggplants with 3–4 zucchini, partially peeled and cut in half lengthwise, and proceed with basic recipe.

variations

· vietnamese stir-fried tofu with basil

see base recipe page 227

stir-fried tofu with cilantro & mint
Follow basic recipe, replacing basil with a small bunch of fresh cilantro and mint leaves, finely chopped.

stir-fried tofu with kaffir lime leaves
Prepare basic recipe, adding 3–4 fresh or dried kaffir lime leaves, crushed in your hand, to wok with marinated tofu. Omit basil leaves.

stir-fried tofu with bean sprouts
Omit basil. Prepare basic recipe and toss in 1/2 pound fresh bean sprouts just before serving.

stir-fried tofu with shrimp
Omit basil. Stir-fry 1/2 pound tiny, shelled shrimp in a little oil and put aside. Follow basic recipe and toss in cooked shrimp just before serving.

stir-fried tofu with peanuts
Prepare basic recipe. Toss in 2–3 tablespoons fresh peanuts, shelled and roughly chopped, with basil.

variations

red thai eggplant curry

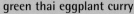
see base recipe page 228

green thai eggplant curry
Follow basic recipe, replacing red curry paste with green Thai curry paste.

red yam curry
Replace eggplants with 2 yams, peeled and cut into bite-size chunks.

green yam curry
Replace red curry paste with commercial green curry paste and the eggplants with 2 medium-sized yams, peeled and cut into bite-size chunks.

red potato curry
Replace eggplants with 12–15 new potatoes, peeled and kept whole.

green potato curry
Replace red curry paste with same quantity of commercial green curry paste. Replace eggplants with 12–15 new potatoes, peeled and left whole.

saigon eggplant curry
Add 1 ounce fresh turmeric root, peeled and finely chopped, to garlic and shallots in wok. Replace red Thai curry paste with same quantity of commercial Indian curry paste. Replace kaffir lime and basil leaves with a small bunch of fresh cilantro, finely chopped.

variations

korean stir-fried potatoes

see base recipe page 231

stir-fried sweet potatoes
Replace potatoes with 2 medium-sized sweet potatoes, peeled and cut into bite-size pieces. Increase soy sauce by 1 tablespoon and proceed with basic recipe.

stir-fried turnip
Replace potatoes with 1/2 pound turnip flesh, cut into bite-size pieces. Proceed with basic recipe.

stir-fried butternut squash
Replace potatoes with 1/2 pound butternut squash flesh, cut into bite-size pieces.

stir-fried pumpkin
Replace potatoes with 1/2 pound pumpkin flesh, cut into bite-size pieces.

stir-fried papaya
Replace potatoes with 2 firm, pink-fleshed papaya, peeled, with seeds removed and cut into bite-size pieces. Proceed with basic recipe, reducing cooking time to 3–4 minutes.

green papaya salad

see base recipe page 232

green mango salad
Replace green papaya with 2 firm green mangos, peeled, pitted, and grated.

green papaya salad with honey
Omit raisins, palm sugar, and cilantro. Stir 2 tablespoons honey into vinegar and proceed with basic recipe.

coconut salad
Replace green papaya with grated flesh of 1 medium-size fresh coconut.

carrot salad
Replace green papaya with 3–4 medium-size carrots, peeled and grated.

daikon salad
Replace green papaya with peeled and grated flesh of 2–3 daikon.

pink papaya salad with lime
Replace green papaya with 2 firm pink papaya (if the flesh is not firm, it will not grate easily, so then dice it finely). Replace coconut vinegar with juice of 1–2 fresh limes.

indonesian mango, pineapple & bean sprout salad

see base recipe page 235

asian pear, pineapple & bean sprout salad
Replace green mango and jicama with 2 Asian pears, peeled, cored, and sliced.

daikon, mango & bean sprout salad
Replace jicama and star fruit with 2 daikon, peeled and sliced.

papaya, pineapple & bean sprout salad
Replace green mango with a small green papaya, peeled, seeds removed, and finely sliced.

ripe mango, papaya & pineapple salad
Replace green mango and cucumber with 1 ripe, but firm mango and 1 ripe but firm papaya, both peeled, with pit and seeds removed, and finely sliced.

mango, bamboo shoot & bean sprout salad
Replace jicama with 1/4 pound bamboo shoots, finely sliced.

banana blossom & bean sprout salad
Replace jicama with hearts of 2 banana blossoms. Cut hearts in quarters lengthwise, slice finely, and soak in water mixed with juice of half a lemon for 20 minutes. Proceed with basic recipe, draining hearts before adding to salad.

variations

japanese bamboo shoot & shiitake salad

see base recipe page 236

korean bamboo shoot & shiitake salad
Add 2 fresh red chiles, seeded and finely sliced, to mushrooms and bamboo shoots. Omit mirin and double quantity of soy sauce.

tofu & shiitake salad
Replace bamboo shoots with 1/2 pound tofu, rinsed and cut into fine strips.

bean sprout & shiitake salad
Replace bamboo shoots with 1/2 pound bean sprouts, rinsed and drained.

cucumber, shallot & shiitake salad
Omit bamboo shoots and add 1 small cucumber, peeled, seeded, and cut into fine sticks, and 2–3 shallots, peeled and finely sliced.

daikon & shiitake salad
Replace bamboo shoots with 2 daikon, peeled and finely sliced.

water chestnut & shiitake salad
Replace bamboo shoots with 6–8 water chestnuts, finely sliced.

desserts &
drinks

To round off a perfect Asian meal, seasonal fruit

such as lychee, mango, and durian is often served.

Sweet desserts and drinks—rice cakes, fried bananas,

sweet bean soups, syrupy beverages, and aromatic

teas—are enjoyed as snacks at any time of day.

asian banana fritters with coconut

see variations page 270

You can be sure to come across deep-fried bananas in your journeys throughout Southeast Asia. Versatile and delicious, they are often munched on their own, sprinkled with sugar, or they can be served with sweet sticky rice, ice creams, or steamed cakes and buns.

1/2 cup all-purpose or rice flour
1 tsp. baking powder
pinch of salt
2 eggs
2 1/2 cups unsweetened coconut milk
scant 1/4 lb. fresh coconut, grated

3–4 large bananas, peeled and halved, then
    halved again lengthwise
vegetable oil
superfine or confectioners' sugar
2–3 tbsp. palm or granulated sugar

Sift flour with baking powder and salt into a bowl. Make a well in center and drop in eggs. Gradually pour in coconut milk, beating all the time, until batter is thick and smooth. Beat in grated fresh coconut, then add bananas, coating them gently with batter.

Heat enough oil for deep-frying in a wok or heavy pan. Check oil is right temperature by dropping in a cube of bread to see if it sizzles and turns golden brown. Work with 2–3 bananas at a time, lifting them out of batter with tongs, or chopsticks, and lowering them into hot oil. Fry until crisp and golden, and drain on paper towel. Sprinkle sugar over bananas and serve while still warm.

Serves 4–6

vietnamese steamed gingerroot custards

see variations page 271

Delicate and warming, gingerroot custard is a great favorite of the Vietnamese and Chinese. Served chilled, the individual custards are often enjoyed as a sweet mid-afternoon or late-evening snack.

1/4 lb. fresh gingerroot, peeled and chopped
1 (14-oz.) can unsweetened coconut milk

4 tbsp. palm or granulated sugar
2 egg whites

Using a mortar and pestle or an electric blender, grind ginger to a fine paste. Press ginger paste through a fine sieve, or twist it in a piece of cheesecloth to extract juice. Reserve juice.

Fill a wok one-third full with water. Place a bamboo steamer in wok, bring the water to a boil, and reduce heat to low.

In a bowl, whisk coconut milk, sugar, and egg whites with gingerroot juice until mixture is smooth and sugar has dissolved. Pour mixture into individual heatproof bowls and place them in steamer. Cover and steam for 15–20 minutes, until mixture sets.

Remove bowls from steamer and let cool. Cover them with plastic wrap and place in refrigerator overnight. Serve chilled or at room temperature.

Serves 4

indonesian sweet black sticky rice

see variations page 272

Throughout Asia, sweet sticky rice, often topped with a little sweetened coconut milk or coconut cream, is one of the most popular snacks. Black sticky rice turns a gorgeous purple when cooked.

1/2 lb. black sticky rice	1 (14-oz.) can unsweetened coconut milk
4–5 tbsp. palm sugar	sea salt
2–3 pandanus leaves or 1 vanilla pod	4 tbsp. shredded coconut

Soak rice grains in water for 4 hours, then rinse and drain. Put rice grains in a pot, cover with 1 1/4 cups water, and bring to a boil. Stir in half the sugar, making sure it dissolves, then add pandanus leaves or vanilla pod. Reduce heat and simmer gently until all the water has been absorbed. Turn off heat, cover pan, and let rice steam for about 10 minutes.

Meanwhile, bring coconut milk to a boil in a separate pot. Stir in remaining sugar, making sure it dissolves. Keep warm over a low heat.

Quickly dry-roast shredded coconut in a small heavy-based pan, tossing all the time, until it gives off a lovely aroma and turns golden brown. Tip into a bowl.

Remove pandanus leaves or vanilla pod from rice, and spoon rice into individual bowls. Drizzle with hot coconut milk and sprinkle each serving with toasted coconut.

Serves 4–6

cambodian baked pumpkin with coconut custard

see variations page 273

In Cambodia and Thailand, this traditional pudding is often served as a sweet snack. Once the custard-filled pumpkin is baked, the flesh is scooped out with the custard and a hot, sweet coconut sauce is drizzled over the top.

1 small, firm pumpkin, cut in half, seeds and
    fiber removed
1 (14-oz.) can unsweetened coconut milk
pinch of salt
3 large eggs
3 tbsp. palm or granulated sugar (plus a little
    extra for sprinkling)

for the sauce
1 generous cup coconut cream
pinch of salt
2 tbsp. palm sugar

Preheat oven to 350°F. Place pumpkin halves, skin-side down, in a baking dish. In a bowl, whisk coconut milk with salt, eggs, and 3 tbsp. sugar, until mixture is thick and smooth like whipping cream. Pour mixture into each pumpkin half. Sprinkle a little extra sugar over top of filling and rim of pumpkin. Place pumpkin halves in oven and bake for 35–40 minutes. Insert a skewer into pumpkin flesh to see if it is tender, and lightly touch custard to see if it feels firm.

Just before serving, heat coconut cream in a pan with salt and sugar. Scoop servings of hot pumpkin flesh with custard into bowls and pour a little sweetened coconut cream over the top.

Serves 4–8

Malaysian sago pudding with palm sugar

see variations page 274

Sago pearls are from the sago palm but look like tapioca. Sago is one of the main staples in Malaysia, where it is used in savory and sweet dishes, such as this one. If you can't find pandanus leaves, use a vanilla pod for flavoring instead.

1 pandanus leaf, tied in a knot
generous 1/2 lb. pearl sago, picked over,
   washed, and drained
1 (14-oz.) can unsweetened coconut milk,
   lightly beaten
sea salt

for the syrup
1 cup water
3/4 cup palm sugar
1 pandanus leaf, tied in a knot

Bring a deep pan of water to a boil. Drop in pandanus leaf. Let sago rain into water through the fingertips of one hand, while you stir with the other to prevent sago from sticking. Boil for 5 minutes, then turn off heat, cover pan, and let sago steam for about 10 minutes—the pearls should become swollen and translucent. Drain sago through a sieve and rinse under running cold water. Discard pandanus leaf and tip sago into a bowl.

Stir in 1–2 tablespoons coconut milk with a pinch of salt—this will give sago a milky appearance. Spoon sago into a lightly greased mold, or 4 separate molds, packing it down gently, and let set at room temperature or in refrigerator for 1 hour. Meanwhile make syrup. Put water and palm sugar into a heavy-based pan and stir over a high heat, until sugar has dissolved. Bring liquid to a boil for 1–2 minutes. Drop in pandanus leaf, reduce heat, and

simmer for 5–10 minutes, stirring from time to time. Keep hot. Beat remaining coconut milk with a pinch of salt—this accentuates the flavor. Tip mold or molds upside down in a shallow bowl and slip them off the puddings. Spoon coconut milk over the top, allowing it to flow down sides and form a pool in dish, then pour over the hot syrup. Eat immediately, while syrup is still hot. (Alternatively, you could keep sago hot in a steamer and heat up coconut milk, so that whole pudding is hot.)

Serves 4

filipino mango ice cream

see variations page 275

This is one of the most popular ice creams in the Philippines, where sweet, juicy mangoes grow in abundance. It is also a great favorite in other parts of Asia, where it is enjoyed at family celebrations and religious feasts.

6 egg yolks
1/2 cup superfine sugar
2 1/4 cups whole or skim milk

1 1/2 cups fresh mango pulp
1 cup whipping cream

In a bowl, whisk egg yolks and sugar together until light and frothy. Heat milk until scalding in a heavy pan, then pour it slowly into egg mixture, whisking constantly. Strain milk and egg mixture back into pan and place it over heat, stirring all the time, until it thickens. Let cool.

Mash mango flesh with a fork for chunky texture, or put it in an electric blender and whiz to a purée. Strain cooled custard into a bowl and whisk in whipping cream. Beat in mango purée until thoroughly mixed, then pour into an ice cream maker. Churn until frozen or, alternatively, pour mixture into a freezer-proof container and freeze for 6 hours, beating with a fork from time to time to break up ice crystals.

Serves 4–6

asian jungle fruits in lemongrass syrup

see variations page 276

This flexible fruit salad is exotic and tropical in flavor—a delicious treat at the end of a Southeast Asian meal. The fruits will vary from region to region and according to the seasons.

for the syrup
1 cup water
3/4 cup sugar
2 stalks lemongrass, bruised

1 firm papaya, peeled, halved, seeds removed, and sliced crosswise
2 small star fruit, cut into stars

1 small pineapple, peeled, sliced into rounds with core removed, and halved
1 can preserved lychee, or 12 fresh lychee, peeled and pitted
2 firm yellow or green bananas, peeled and sliced diagonally
12 mint leaves, roughly chopped

Put water into a heavy-based pan with sugar and bruised lemongrass stalks. Bring liquid to a boil, stirring all the time until sugar has dissolved, then reduce heat and simmer for 10–15 minutes. Let cool.

Put fruit into a serving bowl. Pour syrup, including lemongrass stalks, over fruit. Toss lightly, cover, and chill for at least 6 hours, or overnight, to allow flavors to mingle. Before serving, remove lemongrass. Sprinkle with mint.

Serves 4–6

asian tapioca & coconut soup with banana

see variations page 277

Throughout Asia, this is the type of pudding that everybody's mother or grandmother makes. Sweet and nourishing, it is made with tapioca pearls cooked in coconut milk and sweetened with fruit and sugar.

2 1/4 cups water	scant 1/2 cup sugar
1 1/2 oz. tapioca pearls	salt
2 1/4 cups unsweetened coconut milk	3 ripe bananas, peeled and diced

Pour water into a heavy-based pot and bring to a boil. Stir in tapioca pearls, reduce heat, and simmer for about 20 minutes, until translucent. Add coconut milk, sugar, and a pinch of salt. Cook gently for about 30 minutes, until tapioca pearls are cooked.

Stir in bananas and cook them until soft. Remove pot from heat, spoon soup into individual bowls, and serve.

Serves 4

chinese lychee sorbet with gingerroot

see variations page 278

This type of refreshing sorbet is often enjoyed as a refreshing snack on a hot day, but in restaurants, it is served at the end of the meal or during it to cleanse the palate. Fresh lychees are available in Asian stores and large supermarkets.

1/2 cup granulated sugar
1/2 cup water

1 lb. fresh lychees, shelled and pitted
1 oz. fresh gingerroot, peeled and grated

Put sugar and water into a heavy pan and bring to a boil, stirring all the time until sugar has dissolved. Reduce heat and simmer for 5–6 minutes until syrup coats back of wooden spoon.

Place lychees in a blender with grated ginger and whiz to a purée, or pound smooth with a mortar and pestle. Add syrup and blend until smooth. Pour mixture into a freezer container and place in freezer for about 2 hours, until it has almost set. Beat sorbet to break up crystals, then return to freezer to set.

Serves 4

asian sweet soy milk
with pandanus

see variations page 279

Early in the morning or late at night in Asia, the sight of the soy milk vendor is a welcome one. Served hot or cold, this sweetened drink is very poular throughout the continent.

1 1/2 lb. soybeans, soaked overnight and
　　drained
5 cups water

1–2 pandanus leaves, slightly bruised
2 tbsp. sugar

Put a third of the soybeans into a blender with a third of the water. Blend until thick and almost smooth. Pour mixture into a bowl and repeat with remaining two-thirds. Strain mixture through a fine sieve to extract milk. Discard solids. Rinse sieve and line it with a piece of cheesecloth, then strain milk again. Squeeze cheesecloth to extract all the milky liquid.

Pour squeezed milk into a pot and gently bring it to a boil. Add pandanus leaves with sugar, stirring until sugar has dissolved. Bring mixture to a boil, then reduce heat and simmer for 10 minutes. Ladle hot milk into cups and enjoy sweet, aromatic flavor, or let cool to room temperature and chill in refrigerator.

Makes 2 pints

asian gingerroot & pepper tea with coconut

see variations page 280

Tea infused with ginger is a specialty of the high-altitude regions of Vietnam, Thailand, Malaysia, and Indonesia. It is also the preferred breakfast beverage in the Philippines. It is believed to stimulate the digestion and to be beneficial to one's health.

1 3/4 pints water
1 1/2 oz. fresh gingerroot, peeled and sliced
1 tsp. black peppercorns

1 tbsp. palm or granulated sugar
1/4 lb. fresh coconut flesh, finely shredded

Put water, gingerroot, peppercorns, and sugar into a pot and bring to a boil, stirring until sugar has dissolved. Boil vigorously for 2 minutes, then reduce heat and simmer for 15 minutes or longer. (The tea improves with sitting, so you can make it in advance and reheat it when you want.)

Divide shredded coconut between 4 glasses and strain the hot ginger tea over it. Serve immediately with a spoon to scoop up the coconut.

Serves 4

korean pear & persimmon tea

see variations page 281

The Koreans enjoy drinking a variety of fruit and spice infusions as a digestive after a meal. Generally sweetened with honey, they can be drunk hot or chilled.

3 cups water
2 tbsp. palm or granulated sugar
2 tbsp. honey
1 oz. fresh gingerroot, peeled and sliced

1 Asian pear, peeled, cored, and sliced
2 dried persimmons
1 tsp. pink peppercorns

Pour water into a pot and add remaining ingredients. Bring water to a boil, stirring until sugar has dissolved. Reduce heat and simmer gently for 35–40 minutes until mixture is fragrant.

Strain liquid into cups or glasses and serve hot, or let cool and refrigerate until chilled.

Serves 4–6

variations

asian banana fritters with coconut

see base recipe page 249

asian banana fritters with gingerroot
Replace fresh coconut with 1 1/2 ounces fresh gingerroot, peeled and grated. Proceed with basic recipe.

asian banana fritters with vanilla
Replace fresh coconut with seeds of 1 vanilla pod; extract seeds by slitting pod lengthwise with a sharp knife, then scraping out seeds. Proceed with basic recipe.

asian banana fritters with chocolate
Replace fresh coconut with 1/4 pound dark or milk chocolate, grated. Proceed with basic recipe.

asian banana fritters with coconut & chocolate
Combine grated coconut with 3 1/2 ounces grated dark or milk chocolate. Proceed with basic recipe.

asian pineapple fritters with coconut
Replace bananas with 1 fresh pineapple, peeled, cored, and cut into slices or portions. Proceed with basic recipe.

variations

vietnamese steamed gingerroot custards

see base recipe page 250

asian lemongrass custards
Replace gingerroot with 2–3 fresh lemongrass stalks, trimmed and sliced.
Proceed with basic recipe.

asian orange custards
Omit gingerroot. Add juice and zest of 1 small orange to coconut milk, sugar, and eggs. Proceed with basic recipe.

singapore cinnamon custards
Omit gingerroot. Whisk 1–2 teaspoons ground cinnamon into coconut milk, sugar, and egg mixture, then follow instructions for steaming.

filipino vanilla custards
Omit gingerroot. Beat seeds of 1 vanilla pod into coconut milk, sugar, and egg mixture, then follow instructions for steaming.

indonesian clove custards
Omit gingerroot. Beat 1/2 teaspoon ground cloves into coconut milk and egg mixture, then follow instructions for steaming.

chinese honey custards
Omit gingerroot. Replace palm sugar with 2–3 tablespoons scented honey. Proceed with basic recipe.

indonesian sweet black sticky rice

see base recipe page 252

black sticky rice with gingerroot

Replace pandanus leaves with 1 1/2 ounces fresh gingerroot, peeled and
grated. Proceed with basic recipe.

black sticky rice with nuts

Follow basic recipe. Replace shredded coconut with 2 tablespoons unsalted
peanuts, roughly chopped (and roasted, if you like).

white sticky rice with coconut cream

Replace black sticky rice with white sticky rice. Replace coconut milk with
1 1/4 cups coconut cream and omit shredded coconut. Proceed with
basic recipe.

filipino white sticky rice with vanilla

Replace black sticky rice with white sticky rice. Replace pandanus leaves
with seeds of 1 vanilla pod—slit pod open and extract seeds. Proceed with
basic recipe, omitting shredded coconut.

white sticky rice with mango

Replace black sticky rice with white sticky rice. Peel 2 mangoes and slice
flesh off pit. Follow basic recipe, omitting shredded coconut, and serve with
bite-size pieces of mango.

cambodian baked pumpkin with coconut custard

see base recipe page 253

baked pumpkin with lemongrass custard
Trim and crush 2 lemongrass stalks to extract juice. Beat juice into coconut milk and egg mixture. Proceed with basic recipe.

baked pumpkin with gingerroot custard
Peel and crush 1 1/2 ounces fresh gingerroot to extract juice. Beat juice into coconut milk and egg mixture. Proceed with basic recipe.

baked pumpkin with vanilla custard
Using a sharp knife, slit 1 or 2 vanilla pods lengthwise and extract seeds. Beat seeds into coconut milk and egg mixture and proceed with basic recipe.

baked acorn squash with coconut custard
Replace pumpkin with 2–3 acorn squash, halved crosswise and seeds removed.

baked butternut squash with coconut custard
Replace pumpkin with 2–3 butternut squash, halved lengthwise with seeds removed.

baked pumpkin with vanilla custard & cinnamon
Add seeds of 1 vanilla pod to coconut milk and egg mixture. Proceed with basic recipe until pumpkin is baked and custard has set. Omit coconut cream sauce and dust top of custard with 1–2 teaspoons ground cinnamon instead.

malaysian sago pudding with palm sugar

see base recipe page 254

sago pudding with ginger syrup
Replace pandanus leaf in syrup with 1 ounce fresh gingerroot, peeled and grated.

sago pudding with honey
Replace syrup with 4–5 tablespoons scented honey, melted and runny, so that it pours easily over pudding.

sago pudding with coconut cream
Omit syrup and heat 4–5 tablespoons of coconut cream instead. Sweeten cream with 2 tablespoons palm or granulated sugar and serve with pudding.

sago pudding with puréed mango
Replace syrup with a mango purée (purée a peeled, ripe mango in electric blender).

tapioca pudding with palm sugar
Replace sago pearls with same quantity of tapioca pearls.

tapioca pudding with honey
Replace sago pearls with same quantity of tapioca pearls. Replace syrup with 4–5 tablespoons warmed scented honey.

variations

filipino mango ice cream

see base recipe page 257

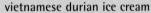

vietnamese durian ice cream
Follow the basic recipe, replacing the mango with the same quantity of durian flesh, whizzed to a purée in an electric blender.

chinese red bean ice cream
Follow basic recipe, replacing mango with same quantity of red bean paste (sold commercially in Asian markets).

banana ice cream
Follow basic recipe, replacing mango with same quantity of banana, mashed with a fork.

thai coconut ice cream
Replace whole milk with same quantity of unsweetened coconut milk. Replace puréed mango with same quantity of shredded coconut. Proceed with basic recipe.

japanese green tea ice cream
Add 2 tablespoons green tea powder (matcha) to scalding milk. Follow basic recipe until custard has thickened, then beat 1 tablespoon tapioca or rice flour mixed with 2 tablespoons milk into mixture until custard coats back of spoon. Omit whipping cream. Transfer green tea custard to a bowl and let cool completely before freezing.

asian jungle fruits in lemongrass syrup

see base recipe page 258

asian jungle fruits in gingerroot syrup
Replace lemongrass in syrup with 1 1/2 ounces fresh gingerroot, peeled and grated. Proceed with basic recipe.

asian jungle fruits in star anise & cinnamon syrup
Replace lemongrass in syrup with 2 cinnamon sticks and 2–3 star anise. Proceed with basic recipe.

asian jungle fruits in clove syrup
Replace lemongrass in syrup with 6–8 whole cloves. Proceed with basic recipe.

mango & coconut in sweet lime juice
Replace fruits with 2 ripe mangos, peeled and sliced, and grated flesh of 1/2 fresh coconut. Omit syrup, and pour juice of 2–3 limes, sweetened with 1–2 tablespoons palm or granulated sugar, over fruit. Cover and chill before serving.

asian pear, lychee & passion fruit
Replace fruits with 2 Asian pears, peeled, cored, and sliced; 12 fresh lychee, shelled and pitted; and the juice of 4–6 fresh passion fruit. Omit syrup and sweeten with 1–2 tablespoons sugar, if you like. Cover and chill before serving.

asian tapioca & coconut soup with banana

see base recipe page 261

asian tapioca & coconut soup with mango
Follow basic recipe, replacing bananas with flesh of 2 ripe mangos, peeled and pitted, and cut into small cubes.

asian tapioca & coconut soup with corn kernels
Proceed with basic recipe, replacing bananas with sweet yellow corn sliced off 2 fresh cobs, or 1 (8-ounce) can drained corn kernels.

asian tapioca & coconut soup with taro root
Peel and dice 1 fresh taro root and add to pot with tapioca pearls. Proceed with basic recipe, omitting bananas.

asian tapioca & coconut soup with sweet potato
Peel and dice 1 medium sweet potato and add to pot with tapioca pearls. Proceed with basic recipe, omitting bananas.

asian sago & coconut soup with avocado
Replace tapioca with sago pearls and proceed with basic recipe. Replace bananas with diced flesh of 2 ripe but firm avocados.

chinese lychee sorbet with gingerroot

see base recipe page 262

lychee sorbet with lemongrass
Replace gingerroot with 1 fresh lemongrass stalk, trimmed and finely sliced. Proceed with basic recipe.

lychee sorbet with lime
Replace gingerroot with zest of 1 fresh lime. Proceed with basic recipe.

mango sorbet with lime
Replace fresh lychees with flesh of 2 ripe mangos. Proceed with basic recipe, replacing gingerroot with zest of 1 fresh lime.

asian pear sorbet with gingerroot
Replace lychees with 2 Asian pears, peeled and cored. Proceed with basic recipe.

asian pear sorbet with lime
Replace lychee with 2 Asian pears, peeled and cored. Proceed with basic recipe, replacing gingerroot with zest of 1 fresh lime.

variations

asian sweet soy milk with pandanus

see base recipe page 265

sweet soy milk with ginger
Follow basic recipe, replacing pandanus leaves with 1 ounce fresh gingerroot, peeled and finely sliced.

sweet soy milk with vanilla
Follow basic recipe, replacing pandanus leaves with 1–2 vanilla pods, slightly bruised to release the flavor.

sweet soy milk with cloves, peppercorns & cinnamon
Follow basic recipe, replacing pandanus leaves with 6–8 whole cloves, 4–6 black peppercorns, and 1–2 cinnamon sticks.

sweet soy milk with lime leaves
Follow basic recipe, replacing pandanus leaves with 4–6 fresh or dried lime leaves, bruised or crushed.

sweet soy milk with mint
Follow basic recipe, replacing pandanus leaves with small bunch of fresh peppermint or spearmint leaves.

sweet soy milk with ginseng
Follow basic recipe, replacing pandanus leaves with 1 ounce fresh or dried ginseng, finely sliced.

asian gingerroot & pepper tea with coconut

see base recipe page 266

asian gingerroot tea with cinnamon
Add 1–2 cinnamon sticks to pot. Omit coconut.

asian gingerroot tea with ginseng
Add 1 1/2 ounces fresh or dried ginseng root, sliced, to pot. Omit coconut.

asian gingerroot tea with shredded papaya
Replace coconut with same quantity of green papaya, peeled and finely shredded.

asian lemongrass tea with coconut
Replace gingerroot with 2 lemongrass stalks, trimmed, cut into 4 pieces and
bruised. Omit peppercorns and serve tea hot or chilled, poured over the coconut.

asian lemongrass tea with shredded papaya
Replace gingerroot with 2 lemongrass stalks, trimmed, cut into 4 pieces, and
bruised. Omit peppercorns and replace coconut with same quantity of shredded
green papaya. Serve hot or chilled.

asian mint tea with lime leaves
Replace gingerroot with a handful of fresh mint and lime leaves and omit
peppercorns. Serve tea hot or chilled, poured over shredded coconut or papaya.

korean pear & persimmon tea

see base recipe page 268

pear & lemongrass tea
Replace dried persimmons with 2 lemongrass stalks, trimmed and bruised.

pear & green mango tea
Replace dried persimmons with peeled and pitted flesh of 1 small green mango.

pear & lime tea
Replace dried persimmons with juice and pared rind of 1 lime. Omit peppercorns.

pear, orange & lemon tea
Replace dried persimmons with juice and pared rind of 1 orange and 1 lemon.
Omit peppercorns.

pear & orange blossom tea
Replace dried persimmons and peppercorns with a handful of fresh orange blossoms for a fragrant flavor.

pear & tiger lily tea
Replace dried persimmons and peppercorns with 1 ounce fresh or dried tiger lilies (the dried ones should be golden in color, or they will taste bitter rather than floral).

index

Note: The following ingredients have not been indexed, as they each occur in the great majority of the recipes: cilantro, garlic, gingerroot, lemongrass palm sugar, scallions, shallots, soy sauce, and vegetable oil.

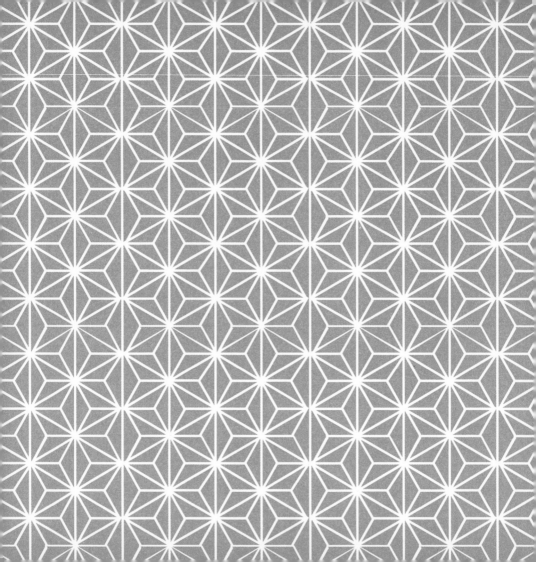